# FROM
# AZEEM
## TO ASHES

JON BERRY

# FROM
# AZEEM
# ᵀᴼ ASHES

## English Cricket's Struggle
## with Race and Class

First published by Pitch Publishing, 2024

Pitch Publishing
9 Donnington Park,
85 Birdham Road,
Chichester,
West Sussex,
PO20 7AJ
www.pitchpublishing.co.uk
info@pitchpublishing.co.uk

ISBN 978 1 80150 882 7

Typesetting and origination by Pitch Publishing
Printed and bound in India by Replika Press Pvt. Ltd.

# Contents

*So there we are, all tangled up together, the old barriers breaking down and the new ones not yet established, a time of transition, always and inescapably turbulent. In the inevitable integration into a national community, one of the most urgent needs, sport, and particularly cricket, has played and will play a great role.*

C.L.R. James in *Beyond a Boundary*

## Brief author's note and disclaimer

This book went into final production in the autumn of 2023, just a few weeks after the compelling Ashes series of the previous summer. The subsequent meltdown of England's 50-over team in the World Cup in India was unfolding as the final proofs were read and so the full details of that debacle are absent from the pages that follow. Sport remains the greatest of unscripted dramas, waiting and sniggering as it turns experts into fools. The most important of life's least important things, always ready to enthral and frustrate in equal measure.

# Introduction

## Sentimentalists beware – this may not be for you

*You may as well go stand upon the beach ... and bid the main flood bate his usual height*

Antonio: The Merchant of Venice

HISTORY HAS given poor old King Canute, or Cnut, to use the dangerously accurate spelling of his name, a pretty unfair press. The idea that he had the power to halt the incoming tide was one that he found absurd; it was his obsequious court followers who came up with the barmy notion that he'd be able to do so. When poor old Cnut sat on the shore getting his socks wet, he was trying to demonstrate the limits of his powers to his dim-witted courtiers, not engage in some vainglorious self-promotion.

Yet however we decide to spell it, his name conjures up the image of a daft old duffer at the seaside, which does him a disservice. His accomplishments were many and varied. His tenure on the English throne – and that of a few Scandinavian countries for good measure – took place in the early years of the 11th century. He was instrumental

9

in drawing up early legislation to settle land disputes, introduced a working currency and forged peace between previously warring northern nations. On balance, he seems to have been a good man and possibly a wise one. He wasn't to know that he would live for a more than a millennium to be mistakenly associated with a futile vanity project.

So, before the pedants reach for the keyboard, I acknowledge that I'm perpetuating this fake news by invoking him. But whatever his motives, and they appear to have been honourable, Cnut was attempting the impossible. The tide will not be held back. This simple premise informs everything that is written in the pages that follow. Sport at every level, but especially at its elite, upper reaches has never been a politics-free zone. The fact that you've picked this book from the shelf or clicked for a peek, probably means that this strikes you as glaringly obvious. But if that's not your view and you're hoping that the wagons can still form a circle and protect cricket, lovely cricket from the grubby reach of the political – and, of course, the economic – world, maybe I can change your mind. I think it best to get that basic intention out there, just in case you were hoping for feeble nostalgia about willow on leather and honey still for tea.

The events dealt with in the pages that follow took place at a time when society had been destabilised by pandemic and war. Hovering over this are existential concerns about the very future of civil, democratic society and even the planet itself. During this time, the conduct of the political class in England, both in the execution of its public duty and the pursuit of its private pleasures, dented confidence in its integrity and ability. What follows places cricket's failings firmly in that broader context. In particular, it suggests that it is unfair and unrealistic to ask cricket alone to solve issues that have their roots in wider societal matters.

Those of us who love cricket do so in different ways. We all want the best of it preserved and protected, while acknowledging that survival means accommodating change. My contention is that trying to understand all of this without wrestling with politics and economics – internal, local and global – is to disarm ourselves during a brutal, commercial battle. So, don't expect any shying away from discussion about the racism, deadening conservatism and plain old class privilege masquerading as untouchable tradition which bedevils the game. There will be no feeble submission to deadening sentimentality or entitlement. There'll be no issuing of useless orders to lapping waves.

Talking of which, let's begin on a sumptuous Caribbean island.

Chapter 1

# Early spring in the Caribbean. It's 29/3 again and Root's captaincy is put out of its misery

*Be not afeard. The isle is full of noises, Sounds, and sweet airs, that give delight, and hurt not.*

Caliban: *The Tempest*

IF ONLY the isle really was full of noises. Unfortunately not, as far as cricket was concerned. It hasn't always been that way, of course. But in the early spring of 2022, there were precious few sweet airs to delight anyone.

On 8 March, in contrast to the dank gloom of an English afternoon, captains Kraigg Brathwaite and Joe Root stepped into the Antiguan sunshine and tossed the coin, resulting in England's decision to bat first. Of the dozens of WhatsApp groups of which I'm either an active member or from which I can't be arsed to unsubscribe, one is composed of friends who follow our twin passions of cricket and football. When it comes to England's Test team, we have a long-standing trope: wherever England are in the world, they're 29/3. At about 2.40 on that grey afternoon, Root played a sort of half-hearted leave at a decent inswinger from Kemar Roach, turned in stunned dismay to see his off stump pinged back and trooped off disconsolately, leaving England 27/3. Dan Lawrence and Ben Stokes eked out two more singles and I reached for my phone but had been easily beaten to it.

What did the home crowd make of this disastrous, if inevitable, start by the visitors? It's a meaningless question. As the England captain made his sheepish way back to the pavilion, there was no barbed jeering, no raucous send-off, no gleeful flag-waving. The guys charged with pumping out forced jollity from the decks and speakers remained stubbornly – almost respectfully – silent. TV camera operators scoured the crowd to find the occasional, isolated local face, possibly waving a flag or raising a can of drink in salute. But Root's dismissal was, for the most part, met with the same sullen, grudging disappointment had it been at Headingley.

Not that the Sir Vivian Richards Stadium in North Sound was empty. Far from it. Most of the fixed seating was occupied and the open spaces on the grass terracing, side-on to the wicket, was gradually filling up as foolhardy sun worshippers staked their claim for the day. Eagle-eyed telly watchers or those like me who've been fortunate enough to watch cricket there, could see the local moms setting up the barbecues, whose fare becomes increasingly irresistible as the effect of Banks's beer kicks in during the day. There are plenty of people watching – it's just that most of them have travelled 4,000 miles to get there.

In the past, I've been one of their number. Despite the hype, most of them (us) are not so much barmy army, more like the reserve unit of Dad's Army. Old, white, retired, financially comfortable and, for the main part, unapologetically conservative in outlook and politics. Once they've been shipped there by travel companies, they're cosseted from hotel to air-conditioned minibus to an evening with Aggers. It's true that there is a less genteel section of England followers than these county stalwarts, but, broadly speaking, both they and this paler constituency represent the lovers of the traditional and the familiar in the game. They'll have paid good money to be at this bland Lego block of a stadium set slap in the middle of the countryside and their dollars will be happily pocketed by locals.

All the same – and numerous conversations bear this out – most of them would prefer to be some seven miles away in the centre of the capital, St John's, watching their cricket in the happily ramshackle Rec – Antigua's legendary Recreation Ground. It was here in 1986 that Viv Richards smashed a Test match century from 56 balls, shredding an England bowling attack that included his mate, Ian Botham – with whom he can be seen exchanging observations of an indeterminate nature at various points during his exploits.

To call Viv Richards the island's favoured son might be a cliché, but there's no doubting its accuracy. In the centre of St John's sits the island's small museum. It is dominated by the interwoven themes of sugar and slavery, the two elements that should make any visitor take stock while enjoying the lavish and fertile beauty of this beach-fringed tourist haven. There's also a bit of geological explanation but apart from that, it's about Viv.

There may be a dozen cricketers who could lay claim to being the ultimate icon of West Indian dominance in the 1980s and 1990s, but few could question the inspirational value of Richards, whose very bearing issued a challenge to his opponents, both sporting and political. The broadcaster and campaigner Darcus Howe, himself the nephew of C.L.R. James, the doyen of Caribbean writers on the game's correspondence with politics, wrote that 'to see Viv Richards walking out to bat at the Oval, which was just down the road from where I lived in Brixton, without a helmet (no matter how fast the bowler was) and wearing his Rasta armbands of gold, green and red, was inspirational.' Richards spoke of how he batted 'for equal rights' and, despite the offer of life-changing sums, was never tempted by so-called 'rebel' tours designed to normalise apartheid in South Africa.

Eight years after his record-breaking century, since superseded by Brendon McCullum and equalled by Misbah-ul-Haq, the Rec was witness to Brian Lara reaching the highest individual score of 375 before going on, a decade later, to overtake Matthew Hayden's subsequent 380 and reach 400. Both of Lara's innings were against England. One can only imagine the weary dread with which that nation's bowlers would have looked forward to encounters there. Their mood would not have been improved by the utterly delirious accolades afforded every boundary by the patrons at St John's – a crowd markedly different from the puffing, perspiring tourists at the future North Sound.

The newer ground – functional, practical and sterile apart from the moms' barbecues – had been built to accommodate games for the 2007 World Cup. An early 'benefactor' of China's belt-and-road investments across the globe, it was constructed at a cost of US$60m. Stark and unloved, such stadia are now all too familiar to football fans uprooted from communities, chip shops and boozers and dragooned to anonymous prefabs in uniform retail parks. And yet, in 2009, unrefined and indecorous St John's, boisterous home to Chickie's Disco and Gravy the cross-dresser, had the last laugh.

On 13 February Andrew Strauss and a lithe Chris Gayle made their way gingerly to the pitch prepared for the start of the second Test at the Sir Vivian Richards Stadium. Although the strip seemed sound, if a touch green, it was clear that neither captain was exactly striding across an outfield that appeared to be largely composed of sand extracted from a nearby beach. Gayle won the toss and asked England to bat. What followed was as comical as it was embarrassing. Jerome Taylor took the new ball and, where one might have expected him to charge in with full fury, he set off like a man plugging through slush in ill-fitting wellingtons, his normally elegant run-up reduced to a stumbling shamble. It took just ten balls for all concerned to decide that the arena was most definitely not fit for purpose and the game was abandoned.

Any follower of cricket is acutely aware that it's a game whose administrators have rarely enjoyed a reputation for being either nimble or imaginative. Not so in the hours that followed the North Sound debacle. Antigua found itself home to two cricket teams and the accompanying media. In contrast to the festival days of Viv's whirlwind knock, when relatively few Brits embraced the atmosphere of the rickety double-decker in the Rec, the island was awash with cricket fans carrying plenty of good folding money. For once, the obvious solution was embraced: back to St John's and the Rec. The move was brilliantly captured in the affectionate observation of journalist, Paul Weaver, who was following the tour for the *Guardian*. 'Anyone asking himself whether the ARG will be ready for today's hastily arranged Test match between West Indies and England should really know better,' he wrote. 'Of course it won't be. It wasn't ready for its first Test match in 1981 and it never suggested anything remotely resembling organised preparedness over the next 25 years, right up to its last Test match in 2006.' As it turned out, the Rec served up a compelling game of cricket, with the hosts holding out for a nervous draw after a game of some 1,500 runs and 36 wickets.

In between Lara's 400, a brief excursion for some World Cup games at North Sound and the return to St John's, the island had also been witness to one of the game's more bizarre episodes. As cricket braced itself for the ground-breaking impact of the Indian Premier League (IPL), Texan fantasist, Allen Stanford, currently residing in the Coleman Penitentiary in Florida where he will be for the foreseeable future, decided that cricket was just the thing he needed to enhance his portfolio. He set about the business of dangling huge sums of money – which he didn't have – in front of credulous and greedy cricketers and their administrators. It didn't end well.

Stanford had acquired the old Airport Cricket Ground in Antigua to use as the base for his adventures. When he landed a helicopter at Lord's with a bag full of fake dollars in 2008, it was entirely in keeping with a man who was there to set up a $20m one-off game between England and his own Superstar XI – a game which turned out to be a complete dud with a ten-wicket victory for the latter. Prior to the action, he had attempted to exercise a kind of cricketing *droit du seigneur* by flirting with England players' wives, a misstep for which he later apologised. By that time, he had already been appointed as a Knight Commander of the Order of the Nation of Antigua and Barbuda, an honour of which he was stripped a few months after the $20m game debacle and the revelation that he was skint and always had been.

To be fair to Stanford, he'll have a tale or two to tell his cellmates, with whom he will share the common complaint that he was framed. On conviction he lamented that his demise 'was caused by wrongful prosecution – an over-zealous and wrongful prosecution'. While this may be familiar territory for the inmates at Coleman, his chosen area of enterprise may be rather more baffling. 'Cricket is not a very big sport in prison,' he observed. Yet, however comedic his Mitty-like attempts to play on the big stage may have been, he was certainly reading the runes about cricket's potential for generating the down-and-dirty dollars which would be driving the short, increasingly dominant, form of the game for the coming decades.

It's probable that much of this history of the island's cricketing heritage would have been known to the paying public in North Sound in March 2022 as Jonny Bairstow marshalled the lower order around his solid century to take England to 311 and a position from which they might have won the game but timidly failed to do so. Having paid good money to watch the longest form of the game, the tension between tradition and the cash cow that preserves it would have been familiar to them all. While most would have been all too content to be sitting in the sunshine enjoying post-Covid liberty, away from Europe's grotesque circus of politics and war, as lovers of the game they'd have been sharply aware that cricket in general was teetering on swampy ground.

The initial shock waves of Azeem Rafiq's revelations and what they exposed about the game may have dissipated temporarily by March 2022, but in many ways a snapshot, literally, of the ground on that Antiguan afternoon would have been illuminating. A good place to start is with the good burghers occupying the best seats.

As already mentioned, I've been of their number. I'm enculturated. I take a flag bearing my name and that of my wife, embellished with the emblem of the football team that has been disappointing me for over 60 years. One of the reasons I take it is so that friends and family can gleefully text me to say that they've seen it. But when it comes to actually spotting me, needles and haystacks don't come into it. I know because I've tried to pick out acquaintances who I know to be in attendance. What identifying features might we be looking for? Ah, yes. White, late middle-age, greying hair, visible if not covered by straw hat or – racy devil – baseball cap, glasses, white polo shirt, possibly half-dozing. What could be more easily identifiable?

If there's homogeneity here, is there more diversity among the players they've come to see? In one respect, the XI who line up for England on this day present a surprise. An oft-cited reason for the small pool in which the game fishes for players is its lack of traction in state schools. Yet from this particular team, only two players – Zak Crawley and Jonny Bairstow – were educated exclusively at private establishments. The captain, Joe Root, moved into the private sector in his teens. The remaining eight all attended state schools, although their biographies clearly reveal that their talent for the game was nurtured at club and county level. In many cases, it is also obvious that strong family links with organised sport will have been the catalyst for their participation outside school. The weighting towards state-educated cricketers in this team is something of an anomaly. In recent years, it has been common for at least half the players in any starting set-up to have been privately educated. The explanation is obvious, but nevertheless I hope the reader will afford me a private intrusion.

I spent the first 30 years of my working life as a schoolteacher, exclusively in the state sector and in comprehensive schools. Apart from my first subject – English, as you may have guessed – I was always happy to help out with running sports teams. When it came to cricket, I was witness to its slow and horrible strangulation in the state sector. Until the mid-80s, I worked in schools which employed ground staff through the local authority. That is, dedicated craftsmen (and it was, as it happens, gender specific) who took time and pride in tending playing fields and for whom the production and maintenance of the cricket square was a source of professional pride. Two deadening factors then intruded and still squat on the game's potential development.

First, grinding annual spending cuts meant that ground staff disappeared to be replaced by careless contractors on tight schedules, allowing for only the most cursory care. Eventually, even the artificial strips brought in to replace real wickets became neglected, overgrown and unusable in any meaningful way. These same spending cuts dictated that cricket equipment, expensive and with a short shelf-life as it passed through so many hands, became another of its victims. Beyond these factors came a school curriculum so obsessed with generating exam results and striving for Ofsted approval, that a time-consuming game, gradually fading from public consciousness and free-to-air TV, became unsupportable and unattractive to pupils and teachers alike.

Such constraints did not, and do not, apply to the private sector. In 2022, *The Cricketer* magazine produced its annual *Schools Guide*. The editor, Huw Turbervill, was keen to praise the schools who had managed to keep the game alive during the pandemic and how it was 'incredibly heartening' to see how many of them had made a comeback after such a difficult period. Acknowledging some unevenness in the development of the game in schools, Turbervill speaks glowingly of how 'what has been consistent across the spectrum is that the dedication to the game in schools has not only remained unaffected, but [has] increased'. The magazine then goes on to list the top 100 senior schools, the best 50 prep schools and, in a nod to modernity, the top 20 all-girls' schools. You only need to remove one batting glove to count the number of non-private establishments in the full 170.

To be fair to Turbervill and his colleagues at *The Cricketer*, they are fully aware of this unbalanced provision and tackle it as an issue in their columns from time to time. Its April 2019 edition presented some stark figures. Of some 4,169 secondary schools in Britain, 286 are independent. Of the 333 schools that submit results and averages to *Wisden*, 87 are from the state sector. Former player, Simon Hughes, reports on a survey conducted in 2017 which revealed that only 12 per cent of secondary school children played cricket on a proper pitch in a four-week period during the school summer term. Former (private school) teacher and *Times* school cricket correspondent Douglas Henderson bemoans the fact that even in the independent sector, counter-productive exam fever cuts across time available for summer sport.

A drive or stroll past any independent school reveals, at a glance, the superior nature of their grounds and facilities. What is not so immediately obvious is the extent to which these are put to use. There is no mandatory time allocation for physical education for state schools in England, merely a suggestion that two hours a week should be dedicated to it. A 2018 survey by the Youth Sport Trust revealed that this two-hour stipulation is largely honoured in state primary schools but rarely achieved at secondary level where some 98 minutes' worth of activity is the norm. The results demonstrated a clear downward trend in time allocated for physical activity. When questioned about the reason for this trend, an emphasis on core subjects and the withdrawal of children from PE for 'interventions' in exam-driven subjects are the most frequently cited reasons.

Meanwhile, over in the private sector, a survey conducted two years earlier for the Headmasters' and Headmistresses' Conference (HMC) revealed a weekly average of 330 minutes played over 40 sports. The report also noted that from the 169 schools that participated, a staggering 1,400 pupils had played for their country across a wide variety of sports. In the distant euphoria following the 2012 London Olympic Games, it was left to the Sutton Trust to point out that one third of GB's medal winners were privately educated, a figure that has remained stubbornly fixed in subsequent Games. Seven per cent of the UK's children go to independent schools.

If the eight fully state-educated players, all of whom were white, who turned out at North Sound represented a slight anomaly in the composition of England's cricket, the nation's footballers consistently hold up a more representative mirror to society. Of the 15 players who took the field for the Euro final at Wembley in July 2021, seven were either black or of mixed heritage. Of the 23-man squad, only one, Tyrone Mings, had been privately educated and that was only a brief, two-year football scholarship at Millfield, something of a breeding ground for sporting success, although not, as scores of lazy editors have learnt to their cost, Ian Botham, who attended Milford Junior School before going on to his local secondary modern and onward to lordly stardom.

So the snapshot at Viv's stadium would have been an illuminating one. A white, well-to-do, ageing set of spectators – many of them stalwarts of their counties and probably reliable supporters of their local clubs – there to watch a team of white cricketers who, even if they hadn't all emerged from private schools, had come through systems patronised by, and familiar to, those who were there to see them. You may think that the following observation may be brusque and unkind stereotyping, but experience tells me that the prevailing manners of the English middle classes at play make it unlikely that conversation in the stands and bars would have been crackling and sparking as they pondered the ways in which the Rafiq affair had put a firecracker under the backside of English cricket. Issues of race and class have a tendency to paralyse this particular constituency. There to watch the start of the red-ball reset and enjoy winter sunshine, they'd have given a wide berth to anyone who wanted to dig into these tangled weeds. And besides, you can't say anything these days, can you?

All of which, admittedly, might be unfair on those who really just did want to watch a bit of cricket in the sun after two miserable and restricted years. Or the minority who were genuinely concerned about the root causes of the game's nagging problems. The unspeakable mess into which English cricket had dug itself hung like a sceptre over proceedings, but live sport is nothing if it not a blinding diversion from the maelstrom of the outside world. This unrepresentative team, followed by a relatively privileged clique in a foreign land, many of whose residents had become indifferent to an expensive and financially inaccessible form of the game, could be unhappily conjoined to stand as a metaphor for cricket's problems. Those problems were manifold and complex and had been bought to the fore by the egregious treatment of a young man who, in other circumstances, could have been the poster boy for progress and diversity in the English game.

## Chapter 2

# Rafiq hits the rough to expose English cricket's frailties

*If the skin were parchment, and the blows
you gave were ink,
Your own handwriting would tell you
what I think.*

Dromio: *Comedy of Errors*

WHEN I embarked on writing this book, I was confident that somebody somewhere would be writing the biography of Azeem Rafiq. It turns out that it's George Dobell, respected and admired in the world of cricket journalism. What follows is not an attempt to tell the same story. Neither is it a blow-by-blow account of a grim saga that brought cricket to the front pages in such an unflattering light: the most casual follower of the game will be familiar with that unedifying chronicle.

But any serious discussion about where cricket finds itself in its country of origin, along with any consideration about how it will develop and for whose benefit, has to start with the series of events that followed this player's revelations and how they were dealt with by the guardians of the game.

On 17 August 2020, some five months after the Covid pandemic took its paralysing grip on the world, journalist Taha Hashim published a feature piece about Rafiq on the *Wisden* website. The central premise seemed to be one that is typical of articles of this sort: promising young cricketer overcomes odds to succeed in the game, is then dogged by injury, circumstance and tragedy but is now steadily rebuilding his life with half an eye on returning to top-level participation. Sad, but all too common.

Hashim traces Rafiq's cricketing story, now familiar to followers of the game, and the wider narrative that has emerged. Having moved from Pakistan to Barnsley in 2001, his obvious talent reaped reward and recognition. Five years later he was captain of England's under-15 team and was given similar responsibility four years afterwards, leading an under-19 team at the World Cup containing Joe Root, Jos Buttler, Ben Stokes and James Vince. By that time, he had made his first-class debut for Yorkshire at the age of 17. In 2012 he captained the county in six T20 games and had made telling contributions to its promotion to Division One of the County Championship.

His subsequent selection for England's Performance Programme tour of India marked the sort of turning point that is regularly documented when young sportsmen fail to fulfil great early promise. Loss of form and a knee injury that stubbornly refused to be fully rehabilitated damaged his progress, particularly in the longer form of the game. 'In terms of white-ball cricket,' Rafiq told Hashim, 'I was still up there; it was more I lost complete confidence in my red-ball cricket and that started to take its toll on both formats.'

There followed a few stumbling years with Rafiq eventually making a mark as a white-ball specialist for Yorkshire until he was floored by the sledgehammer of awful personal tragedy.

Rafiq tells Hashim of receiving a phone call in May 2018, while playing in a one-day game against Warwickshire, and hearing of the stillbirth of his son. He hints at enduring resentment at how this was handled by his employers, especially as his contract with the county was terminated some months later. 'That's for another day,' he tells the journalist. He refers to the excellent assistance he received from the Professional Cricketers' Association and to the personal support from fellow professionals, singling out Adil Rashid for particular praise. At that point, as Hashim explains to his readers, 'it's a story involving Rashid ... that sees this interview takes a turn'. It became a turn that put a bomb under English cricket, the damage from which – along with the efforts to repair it – informs much of what follows in this book.

The story, now much repeated in media coverage, involves him walking out to play around the time of his debut for Yorkshire in 2008. He tells of taking the field with three other players of South Asian heritage – Rashid, Ajmal Shahzad and Rana Naved-ul-Hasan. He recalls how 'one player' mentioned that 'there's too many of you lot – we need to have a word about that'. That 'one player' was alleged to have been former England captain, Michael Vaughan, who has vehemently denied ever speaking in this way. Rafiq goes on to reference comments by former England opener, Michael Carberry, just a few weeks previously. He had been talking to the *Cricket Badger* podcast about the racism rife in the game. Excusing the two most prominent England players of colour, Rashid and Moeen Ali, from publicly expressing a view because they are 'in the set-up', Carberry talked of endemic racism in the game and of how speaking out is riven with problems. '[It's] a decision most Black people and people of colour have to make all the time ... this thing is eating you inside every single day with what you hear in dressing rooms, what you see, the stuff people get away with and say to you.' Rafiq echoes this regret at not having spoken out. 'I've been in that system for nearly the best part of two decades,' he tells Hashim. 'I know how it works [but] I'd love to see change.' At that point, he would have been unaware of the gathering storm he was about to unleash.

The interview had not turned out to be the routinely sorry saga of unfulfilled promise that Hashim may have intended. A week later, *Cricket Badger*, picking up on the link between the comments of Carberry and Rafiq, brought the latter to the microphone. The host of the programme is James Buttler. Affable, intelligent and open-minded, he was once the press officer for Yorkshire Cricket Club. He expresses what comes across as genuine regret and surprise, along with a measure of self-admonishment, when he talks of how he had been blind to the racism that had bedevilled his guest. It is this very obtuseness, a kind of grotesque enactment of a three-wise-monkeys approach to racist behaviour, that was to surface with grim regularity over the next few months. One senior figure after another took their turn to express their astonishment that their beloved game could be so besmirched. It was about to cost some of them dear.

If Buttler is thoughtful and measured in his comments about the racism Rafiq endured, the cricketer himself is now less temperate. He is angry, raw and determined to address injustice. The tragedy of the stillbirth haunts him. He makes no direct connection between this and the slide of his professional career but there is no escaping the misery he endured during this period. He recalls slurs, jibes and insults and has no time for the perpetually lame recourse of the jockocracy to the panacea of 'banter'. Although the interview ends with reference to the birth of a healthy child and the establishment of a newly flourishing business, there is no doubting Rafiq's determination to right wrongs and to call out some culprits.

By the first week in September 2020, cricket journalists were seeking him out as the hottest interview property in the game. George Dobell followed up on the work of Hashim and Buttler for a piece on *Cricinfo*. Rafiq reiterated much of what he has already told them, although going further when talking of how thoughts of suicide had occurred to him. Dobell's report of the interview is a selective edit, not a full audio transcript, but by then Rafiq seems to have done two things since his initial conversation with Hashim for *Wisden*.

First, any hesitancy at laying the blame on the institutional racism infecting Yorkshire cricket and the game more widely, has now entirely evaporated. 'Let me make it really clear,' he tells Dobell. 'I am talking about Yorkshire. I believe the club is institutionally racist and I don't believe they are prepared to acknowledge the fact or willing to change.' Second, his successive interviews seem to have hardened his resolve: there is something of the Rubicon in his observations by September that there will be no timid appeasement. 'I know what I'm doing here,' he confirms. 'I know that by speaking out I'm damaging my chances of working in the game again … but I also know it's the right thing to do and if I have to stand alone to do it, I will.' That undiminished resolve to call out racism became the hallmark of his conduct during the months that followed.

In choosing this path, he may have been unaware of the predictable dynamic that was about to emerge in some quarters. There developed a prevailing discourse that the spinner did protest too much; that he was reading too much into the regulation misfortunes, missteps and careless throwaways that are the fabric of any workplace. Especially when that workplace was the testosterone-charged arena of male sporting endeavour. Giving succour to those who sat in that camp was the revelation of an exchange of messages in the autumn of 2011 between Rafiq and fellow professional, Ateeq Javid, furnishing an example of just such careless prejudice.

It is an ugly episode. Shortly after Rafiq's subsequent testimony to the Department for Digital, Culture, Media and Sport (DCMS) select committee in parliament in November 2021 – to which we will return – it was revealed that he had accused a third player of being reluctant to spend money at a team dinner because 'he is a Jew'. The message is then compounded when he suggests that the player would steal his second helpings as 'only Jews do that sort of shit'. In one respect, Rafiq got off lightly. Given their propensity to identify even the faintest whiff of anti-Semitism, real or imagined, coming from their political opponents, the heads of Jewish organisations were quick to recognise a genuine victim of discrimination and were happy to accept his fulsome apology and to write off his actions as youthful indiscretions. The president of the Board of Deputies of British Jews, Marie van der Zyl, acknowledged that he had 'suffered terribly at the hands of racists in cricket' and that his 'apology seems heartfelt and ... completely sincere'.

And so, with dispiriting predictability, it was left to Nigel Farage to take to Twitter to pronounce that 'Azeem

Rafiq is guilty of the worst double standards possible' before going on to whiningly demand that 'we please end this attempt to destroy English cricket.' Whether the self-appointed champion of saying the unsayable could have been speaking for anyone is impossible to assess. Writing in the online *sportsgazette* shortly after the revelation, journalist Arif Islam captured the utter irrelevance of using Rafiq's disgraceful indiscretion to deflect from the seriousness of what had been revealed by his testimony. 'It brings to light,' wrote Islam, 'the unfortunate truth that there are still many who believe that people of colour in Britain "play the race card" to exaggerate hardship, and that systemic racism is nothing but a myth.'

I have no insight into what measures, training or professional development may have since been instigated by the England and Wales Cricket Board (ECB) to address the issues raised by Rafiq's revelations. Neither am I sure that recommendations for background reading would have been part of their approach. Which would be a shame, because the best thing the board could have done would have been to have plonked a copy of Reni Eddo-Lodge's excellent bestseller, *Why I'm No Longer Talking to White People About Race*, on the desk of every county chairman in the country. If those individuals could then steer themselves past any initial frothing resistance, they'd soon be rejecting the flimsy race-card argument and recognising its inadequacy to explain away anything.

'I can no longer engage with the gulf of an emotional disconnect that white people display when a person of colour articulates our experiences,' writes the author. 'You can see their eyes shut down and harden. It's like treacle is poured into their ears, blocking up their ear canals like they can no longer hear us.' She points to the inability of those who have never understood the advantages and privileges that ensue simply from being white and their 'bewilderment and defensiveness as they try to grapple with the fact that not everyone experiences the world in the way that they do'. She bemoans the fact that whenever events align to remind them of the innate, systemic inequality this generates, and from which they unwittingly benefit, their reaction is to 'interpret it as an affront'.

If the written observations of a 32-year-old woman whose cricketing credentials prove unpersuasive – Google searches reveal no hidden abilities to bowl the carrom ball – then maybe a brief video from one of the game's genuine legends could be a way of easing refusers into the argument. A few weeks before the Rafiq interviews and in the wake of growing protest following the death of George Floyd, Sky Sports broadcast an interview with Michael Holding, speaking to fellow commentators and former players, Ian Ward and Nasser Hussain, during a break in play in a ghostly, behind-closed-doors Test match against the West Indies in Southampton. It is a verbal volley that's up there with any of his fiercest spells.

'They keep on telling me there's nothing called white privilege,' Holding growls with exasperation. 'Give me a break.' He is just as impatient with lame 'get over it' arguments when speaking of historic wrongs – and his range of references and examples flow with fluent incandescence. The middle eastern Jesus universally depicted with pale skin, blond hair and blue eyes; the airbrushing from history of Lewis Howard Latimer, who invented the light-bulb filament but whose fame is obscured by that of Thomas Edison; the immediate suspicion from security guards when

Black people enter open-plan shops. He invokes the all-pervasive, corrosive racism that seeps determinedly into every aspect of life for Black people. Like Rafiq, he talks of having been silent long enough. As a player, his hard-edged focus on dislodging batters to the exclusion of any verbal engagement had been legendary. There is no such cold-bloodedness here; Whispering Death is an angry man with something to say.

His brief interview did not evaporate into the ether: his was a voice to which the Black sporting world was keen to listen. His subsequent award-winning volume, *Why We Kneel, How We Rise* was generated after immediate contact from a range of prominent Black sportspeople urged him to take the argument further and to a wider audience. Having seen the interview, the footballer Thierry Henry immediately called him and urged him to 'keep talking'. From there Holding undertook the project that elicited testimony from, among others, Usain Bolt, Michael Johnson, Makhaya Ntini and Naomi Osaka, all of whom testified to the destructive current of racism that they had endured during their lives on and off the field of play.

So it was that Azeem Rafiq's initial interview for a cricket website catering for a limited, niche readership, set in train a debate about cricket and race that chimed harmoniously with society's wider concern about racism and equality. In doing so, it exposed to public view the narrow layer of society that had contentedly and uninterruptedly been running the game in England at senior level for over a century. More specifically, it was that expression of dull conservatism that holds sway in oak-lined cricket pavilions from Lord's to villages from Ludlow to Leigh that found itself under unwanted scrutiny. Loyally answerable to the members and wallowing in its learned behaviours, events were about to make these honest citizens take a close and uncomfortable look at themselves.

Rafiq's comments detonated an explosion and from the resultant rubble, English cricket had been set the challenge of repairing itself. The broad picture from what ensued is all too easily recognisable for anyone with even a passing interest in how public life is conducted in modern Britain. There emerges a grimly comic cycle of denial, obfuscation, delay and grudging acceptance, all executed in the latent hope that we can soon find ourselves back with good old comfy denial again before you can notice it.

In October 2020, Yorkshire appointed an independent panel operating under the auspices of the Independent Commission for Equity in Cricket (ICEC) and chaired by Dr Samir Pathak. A registrar specialising in liver and pancreatic surgery, Pathak had played cricket for English Universities in 2004 and had been instrumental in establishing Cricket Beyond Boundaries in 2011, a scheme developed to provide support for young cricketers some of whom, but by no means all, came from difficult backgrounds. Joined by, among others, employment lawyer, Rehana Azib and head of HR at Waitrose, Helen Hyde, the panel operated, fittingly, at Boycottian speed. Despite efforts by Rafiq's legal advisers to up the run rate, it was not until the following August of 2021 that anything approaching official findings were released.

On Saturday, 14 August, just as the pride of Yorkshire football, Leeds United, were getting thumped 5-1 on the opening day of the season by Manchester United, the independent panel delivered its 100-page report to executives at Headingley. By the following Wednesday, the club was still holding on to it and, unsurprisingly, Rafiq took to social media to proclaim the whole business 'a sham'. With uncharacteristic purposefulness, the ECB intervened, and chairman Ian Whatmore demanded that Yorkshire provide the board with a copy as well as setting a date for full publication. 'It has taken considerable courage for Azeem Rafiq to speak out,' said Whatmore, 'and it is right that his experiences should have been thoroughly investigated.' He demanded that the ECB 'as the ultimate regulator of the game' be in receipt of the findings.

Unmoved by these requests, Yorkshire's stout denizens held on to the full report before issuing a summary nearly a month later. In the lame hope of burying bad news, the club released its statement on the day when the fifth Test against India had been called off because of Covid infections and most definitely not because the players didn't want to jeopardise their IPL contracts.

Seven of the 43 allegations identified by Rafiq's legal team were upheld, but the panel was unable to prove the existence of institutional racism because of insufficient evidence. Furthermore, no individuals were directly identified and neither were any of their specific actions condemned. The panel cited concern about 'privacy law and defamation' as justification for this reticence. Club chairman, Roger Hutton, voiced sincere apologies for the hurt caused to Rafiq and his family, although later developments suggested that he was far from content with this measly response. Within a matter of weeks, he had resigned his post at Yorkshire, having called out various colleagues for their actions and attitudes. He went on to express the unequivocal view that the club was, indeed, institutionally racist.

Condemnation for the tardy, evasive reaction from an organisation that was clearly in deep denial was widespread. The player's representatives articulated dissatisfaction with 'the atrocious way this process continues to be handled'. The ECB, frustrated as it continued to wait for the full report to drop on its doormat, offered its own apology and reiterated the view that there was no place for racism in the game. Their sentiments were reinforced, almost suspiciously verbatim, by the Professional Cricketers' Association as they were, rather more independently, by Julian Knight MP, the chairman of the DCMS committee.

Perhaps uncharacteristically in a world where the double-speak of parliamentarians has become increasingly normalised, the honourable member's comments were more forthright and purposeful than those in the cricket world itself. Knight berated the club for not being 'willing to publish its findings' and having 'been pressed into doing so'. He detected a 'lack of genuine contrition in [the] statement', insisted that individuals be named and emphasised how critical it was that the club now acted 'with the utmost transparency and speed'.

Knight was to play a central part as events unfolded during the autumn of 2021. MP for comfortable Solihull, he recaptured the seat from the Lib Dems in 2015 and sits on a number of all-party parliamentary committees – the places where, insiders will tell you, the real work tries to get done. He's a bit of a mixed bag for a prominent Tory. State-educated and with a modest degree from a red brick university, he is a Remainer and critical of plans to privatise Channel 4. As a former BBC journalist, he is not a supporter of the licence fee in its current form and has written books on tax avoidance.

Another of his literary endeavours is *Cricket for Dummies*, a perfectly likeable introduction to the game. He's aware enough to excuse the use of the male pronoun throughout – it was published before the ubiquity of 'batters' and 'third' – and although he acknowledges the complexity of the game, he makes the bold claim that before long the reader is 'going to be transformed into a cricket expert'. As a member of the all-parliamentary committee on cricket, as well as being chair of the DCMS, he was a man with a dog in the fight as he took his seat in the committee room on Tuesday, 16 November 2021.

Even before the hearing, events had moved on. A week or so earlier, Yorkshire had opted to offer a six-figure sum in order to settle Rafiq's employment tribunal case without recourse to procedure. By then, the club's stewardship had changed, with Kamlesh Patel – Lord Patel of Bradford – having succeeded Roger Hutton who, unlike chief executive Mark Arthur and director of cricket Martyn Moxon, had felt which way the wind was blowing and lost any appetite he ever had for defending the indefensible. In announcing the settlement, Patel, who referenced the daily racism he personally had experienced throughout his life, spoke of his resolve to address the changes needed if the county was to produce the next Joe Root, Virat Kohli or Babar Azam. 'I am determined to make this club the beating heart of English cricket again,' he announced. 'After 158 years … we're ready to accept the past and become a club which people can trust to do the right thing.'

So by the time Azeem Rafiq came to give his full and emotional testimony to Knight and his committee, the ground had, perhaps, begun to shift a little. Not that this made listening to his evidence any more comfortable. Under parliamentary privilege, names – some of them with high profiles in the game – were named and their actions called out. A culture, both at Yorkshire and within the wider county game, was exposed. It was one in which the use of the terms 'Paki', 'elephant washer' and 'waiter' – disciplinary offences themselves in most modern workplaces – were commonplace. There would have been no use in complaining about any of this or the whole raft of minor, throwaway incivilities and discriminatory acts, Rafiq explained, because 'no one felt it was important'.

Notwithstanding its impact on the panel and the watching public, Rafiq's compelling testimony served to underline much of what had already been leaked, hinted at or greedily dissected in social media. It was confirmation, rather than news, with a few heavyweight names included for a bit of depth and colour. His tearful comments were, rightfully, good copy. Unsurprisingly, they gobbled up the column inches at the expense of a couple of less sensational, but hugely relevant, episodes.

The first of these emerged as Knight, although entirely scrupulous about allowing Rafiq his voice, attempted to establish a wider context for his comments. In doing so, he exposed something of the web of connections through which those in power watched each other's backs. This began when he criticised Arthur and Moxon for failing to accept their invitations to attend: the latter was suffering from stress and the former just didn't seem to fancy it. It was left to Roger Hutton, no longer burdened by office, to face the committee. Cricket's renowned mate-ship wasn't much in evidence.

His former colleagues weren't there, explained Hutton, because they were 'unable to accept the gravity of the situation'. When asked why he hadn't made moves to address their possible removal, Hutton claimed that he was hamstrung by the fact that the Graves Family Trust was owed more than £15m by the club and had a veto on board members. Colin Graves was formerly chair at the ECB and executive chair at Yorkshire. He, too, had refused an invitation to speak to the DCMS committee, although had not been so reticent about privately briefing a local journalist to downplay the importance of the role of the trust.

All of this spoke of the routine machinations of people accustomed to notional wealth and brief authority, who use these attributes to gain and perpetuate influence. Nowhere was this bluff world of the privileged more in evidence than when Rafiq was questioned by committee member, Damian Green MP – and here I'm indebted to the work and the sharp eyes and ears of the consistently admirable journalist, Jonathan Liew, for spotting this. If things were so very bad at Yorkshire, Green wanted to know, why on earth did Rafiq want to carry on working for them? It was a question similar to that posed by the ever-affable Aggers on the radio that very morning.

'The law, in its majestic equality,' wrote Anatole France some hundred years ago, 'forbids rich and poor alike to sleep under bridges, beg in the streets and steal loaves of bread.' Whether or not Green and Agnew would spot the ironic intent of the comment is between themselves and their intellect. The former's relationship with crude cash is more fully on public record than that of the latter. Despite living some 45 minutes away from Westminster, Green was found to be claiming mortgage and council tax expenses for a second home in Acton, west London. But then, he's a man with a thick skin. He's had the indignity of being arrested in his own home for aiding and abetting misconduct in public office, has an unwanted reputation for being touchy feely with the laydeez and for having a sneaky Google for Sexy Suzie on his work laptop. Why on earth, he asks cricketer

Azeem Rafiq, who has one job, one home and one wife, did you keep going back to work?

Surely, if a chap doesn't like one job, he can take another. The old cliché is that the Church of England is the Tory party at prayer. A stroll round the periphery of Lord's on the day of a Test match is to reformulate this maxim: for most of those charged with running the game, cricket is the Tory party at play. There may well be plenty of ordinary punters (like me) who've bitten the bullet of absurd ticket pricing to enjoy a day's cricket, but we're swamped by a different breed. The dozers and dribblers might remain slumped in the Long Room, but easy-going wealth hangs in a haze of exclusive after-shave over the crowds round the pavilion entrance and adjoining manicured enclosures. In fitted Panamas and elegant linen, in aviator shades and strawberry corduroys, in designer frocks and beribboned bonnets, they sway and bray as they carelessly swipe for bubbly or Pimm's. The former players and panjandrums bear themselves with the bronzed confidence gleaned from golf courses, country retreats and, of course, afternoons at the cricket. The need for a regular day job and the pay that goes with it flits round the edges of such privileged lives.

Azeem Rafiq's decision to speak out lit a fire under the governance of English cricket. Issues of race and class that had either been ignored or airbrushed from their consciousness, could no longer be airily dismissed or overlooked. By the time England were 29/3 on that first morning at North Sound, the roll call of fallen heads was lengthy. Following the departure of Roger Hutton, Hanif Malik and Stephen Willis followed him out of the Yorkshire boardroom door. The reticent Mark Arthur, along with fellow absentee official, Martyn Moxon, were on their way, as was first team coach, Andrew Gale.

Across the Pennines, fan-favourite, David Lloyd, whose words and actions had been criticised by Rafiq, decided it was time to step away from the microphone and Michael Vaughan's phone stopped ringing for media engagements. In a further development, Yorkshire and Headingley were to be deprived of the lucrative privilege of hosting international matches. Tom Harrison was still clinging tentatively to office as the CEO of the ECB, but by the time a weary Joe Root had come home and decided that the cross of captaincy was one he no longer wished to bear, Harrison too was no longer in lofty office.

Chris Silverwood had already paid the price for England's lame Ashes surrender and the comfy punters in Antigua could be excused for thinking that talk of the red-ball re-set might have been overplayed as his temporary stand-in, the redoubtable Paul Collingwood, failed to stir any match-winning heroics from his fragmented and depleted charges. Within a few weeks, Rob Key was in place as managing director of English cricket and Brendon McCullum as head coach of the Test team. Darren Gough took over the coaching role at Yorkshire and was joined by Steve Harmison and Ryan Sidebottom. By then, interim chair of the ECB, Barry O'Brien had already announced £25m of strategic funding over five years to sustain the 'action and improvements [that] will be required over months and years if we are to become the most welcoming and diverse sport in the country'. And when the focus eventually returned to the field of play, the unwavering positivity of new England meant that the administrators could breathe a little easier as they vacated centre stage.

## Chapter 3

# Yorkshire in the spotlight. Biffing Jonny and silky Joe almost cover the stain

*Made glorious summer by this son of York*

King Richard: *Richard III*

ON 27 June 2022, at just after half past two on a dull Leeds afternoon, Jonny Bairstow plonked another Michael Bracewell pie six rows back into the terracing to complete a seven-wicket win over New Zealand. For the third consecutive Test match, England had been set over 250 to win in the fourth innings and for the third consecutive Test match they had done so with confident ease. No side had ever accomplished such a feat, the numbers for which are astonishing. In those three chases, they scored 874 runs for the loss of 13 wickets and did so at a rate of 3.5 runs per over. There may have been a sedate crawl to 296 in 117 overs at Lord's for the first game, but the subsequent contests at Trent Bridge and Headingley saw England's batters bash along at a rollicking average of 4.5. Of those 874 chasing runs, 427 were scored by Bairstow and his fellow Yorkshireman, Joe

Root, to add to the combined 363 first-innings totals they had compiled. A compelling combination of 4-by-4 flatbed truck and sleek Rolls-Royce.

In a series characterised by the good-natured fellowship of players who now play with each other around the globe, the usual vagaries of the game applied in bucketloads. Catches dropped at crucial moments, along with some clumsy usage of the review system, could have contributed to different outcomes. New Zealand were the victims of the soul-destruction that is the taking of a wicket – and a key one at that – from a no-ball. There were injuries during the game to bowlers and the loss of their captain, Kane Williamson, to Covid, only for his sublime run-scoring talents to desert him when he did get to play. Stubbornly competitive, they contributed to a genuinely engaging series with some wonderful cricket of their own, but, overall, looked somewhat tired and jaded and, apart from a devastating half-hour from Trent Boult, their bowling lacked real zip. But, to borrow from the wit and repartee of the dressing room, if my auntie had bollocks, she'd be my uncle, and nobody disputed England's status as worthy victors.

From time to time, the TV cameras would direct their gaze to the England balcony where a permanent fixture was the new coach, Brendon McCullum – Baz – lounged in draped insouciance, enacting a chiropractor's nightmare of poor sedentary posture. His expression, whatever the match situation, always seemed to be one of benign contentment, and if there were any in-play interventions on his part, they had all been conducted away from the intrusion of the long lens. Along with praise for England's newly appointed Test captain, Ben Stokes, the commentariat and their informed insiders were unanimous in their recognition of his contribution to the new mindset that England's players, and their batters in particular, had brought to the series. Most intelligent commentators, as well as regular England watchers, were far too percipient to start spouting guff about new dawns and bright new futures, but plenty of paying punters, including those who had returned with lighter wallets from the no-shows of the Caribbean, might have allowed themselves a sliver of optimism for the tougher tests, literally, to come. They weren't to know that one of these would set the stage for the two Yorkshiremen to outstrip their accomplishments a few weeks later.

A few hours prior to Jonny bunting the red-ball team to speedy victory, McCullum's mate and former colleague, Eoin Morgan, indicated that he was calling it a day as England's one-day, white-ball captain. If Baz was at the start of a project to revitalise the approach to the long game, his mate could reflect on half a dozen years in which he had been indisputably central in transforming an embarrassing clutch of underperforming no-hopers into genuine world-beaters. The implication, as cricket lovers basked in the unfamiliar contentment of three England wins on the bounce, was that positivity, bravery and the banishment of fear of failure would be the hallmark of Stokes's England. The spectres of the Gabba and the Wankhede might well be lurking and smirking, but for the moment, in the shadow of the white rose, things were looking up.

There must have been plenty of smug contentment up in the boardroom too. While the official Yorkshire CC Twitter feed gleefully chirruped about the wonderful game Headingley had just hosted, and club officials basked in the approval of following Nottinghamshire's admirable example of staging the last day free of charge, they might also have been slumped with relief. They'd pulled off the double heist of burying bad news while also slipping past the jailer.

At the start of November 2021, the ECB had announced the suspension of Headingley as an international host. As a firm statement of principle, it made a significant impact: it was a grave and far-reaching punishment. I might be unfairly characterising the membership of the ECB and the newly constituted management of Yorkshire cricket, but I'm going to hazard an informed guess that they are probably traditionalists of a small c conservative nature. As such, they'll be in favour of notions of proportionate penalties commensurate with, and proportionate to, the offence committed. Given this assumption, any dispassionate assessment of the sanctions meted out to their county would have told them that, quite frankly, they'd been granted a perfectly fair and proper sentence.

The ECB, showing awareness of the crisis on its doorstep, made it clear that the club was 'suspended from hosting international or major matches until it has clearly demonstrated that it can meet the standards expected of an international venue, ECB member and first-class county'. The same statement made reference to the 'serious damage to the reputation of the game' caused by Yorkshire's actions – or, more precisely, inactions – and asserted that 'there is no place for racism or any form of discrimination in cricket'. As a consequence, the board's subsequent retraction on 11 February 2022, exactly 100 days later, seemed as lenient as it was precipitate.

Just for absolute clarity, during these 100 days, no cricket was played out of doors in England. Put another way, any measures that Lord Patel and the new regime intended to put in place were entirely notional. It was a Yorkshire pudding, the eating of which was yet to be undertaken: fine words, as they say in those parts, butter no parsnips ... and, yes, I'll leave off with these shocking culinary references forthwith. The club's professed determination to face up to its failures, and the acknowledgement of Patel and his team that there was much to do, had been enough for the ECB to relent, even before the first portly medium-pacer had decided that the days were beginning to lengthen and he'd better look out his gym kit.

Barry O'Brien was the interim director at the ECB, and he commended Patel and his colleagues for their work so far. There were many reasons, he explained, to welcome Headingley back into the fold. Among these, he gave precedence to 'the impact on fans who have bought tickets in good faith and the young people who will benefit from Yorkshire's improved outreach and pathway provisions'. To every strict parent and stern schoolteacher – and I include myself in both categories – it looked like a cat had been gleefully let out of the bag. Yes, you've done terrible wrong here. Yes, you need to be firmly punished for so doing. But, but, but ... it's just the tiniest bit inconvenient for all of us and it may work to our disadvantage, so, go on then: we've made our point – just make sure you learn from it. And don't do it again.

A few weeks after the reprieve, Yorkshire's marketing optics took another positive turn. In November 2021, Emerald Publishing, who had previously enjoyed the naming rights at the ground, cut all ties with the club because of the racism scandal. By the start of April 2022, their place had been taken by the conveniently named Clean Slate Studio, an Indian digital streaming company, committed, they claim, to being a 'female-forward' organisation with a mission to challenge gender stereotypes in Indian film and a promise to make Headingley 'a flagbearer for inclusivity and diversity in cricket'. The company is sprinkled with some mega-stardust from both India's big screen and, by association, its cricketing demigod. Clean Slate is the creation of Karnesh Sharma and his sister Anushka – one of the principal stars of Hindi cinema and wife of Virat Kohli. For Patel and those around him, it was a good look. Azeem Rafiq had already announced himself pleased with the lifting of the ban and expressed optimism about the new sponsors. 'The name is one thing, but it is everything else from now on that happens that is important,' he explained, before going on to express the hope that local kids would walk past the ground 'and think this is my club'.

Joe and Jonny leading the victory charge. The ban lifted and a Clean Slate all round. Azeem magnanimously wishing everyone well. An eminent person of colour in charge of a board that looked increasingly more representative of the local community. The sons of York were, surely, well on the way to making amends and even, perhaps, in the forefront of the drive to making the game more diverse and inclusive. Not quite.

Even the buccaneering spirit of Baz and Stokes, followed by the warm fuzz of Morgan's retirement and his glorious memories, could not suppress the turmoil that still bubbled around Yorkshire. Shortly before the third Test in Leeds, David Willey, the captain of the T20 team, announced that he would leave the county at the end of the season. At the time, he was playing for England's white-ball team in a jolly over in the Netherlands – an activity which was all part of the fever-dream chaos that was the English season's fixtures, to which we will return. While Darren Gough and Yorkshire publicly suggested a dispute over wages and contracts was at the root of the affair, Willey took a different, if rather oblique, view. 'The cricket and the current players seem to be secondary at the current moment to repairing the club's reputation,' he wrote on Instagram.

A few days later, Tom Kohler-Cadmore followed in Willey's footsteps. He played a much straighter bat on social media, confining his comments to the regulation platitudes of thanking former colleagues and looking forward to new opportunities. Reports, uncorroborated but widespread, suggested that his father, Mick, a dressing-room attendant, had previously left the club, unhappy about the clear-out of backroom staff that had followed the Rafiq testimony. In the brief gap between the Headingley Test and the clunky resumption of the India series at Edgbaston, another of the victims of that clear-out, former captain and coach, Andrew Gale, added to the ever-rumbling storm with a biting set of comments that provided stark contrast to the comparative reserve of Willey and Kohler-Cadmore.

Three weeks earlier, an employment judge, Joanna Wade, ruled that Gale's 'complaints of unfair dismissal' from Yorkshire had been 'well founded'. At that point no necessary compensation to which she alluded had been finalised, but her ruling emboldened an aggrieved Gale to take a defiant stance towards the ECB. On 29 June, he announced that he would not be engaging with the board's disciplinary process because he had 'no faith that a fair and just outcome will be the result'. He dubbed the board's approach 'tainted' before going on to deny any racist comment, behaviour or attitudes on his part. If Willey and Kohler-Cadmore had been coy, Gale was not holding back. 'Lord Patel saw fit to place Azeem on a pedestal and immediately lost face as

Azeem's anti-Semitic language came into the public domain,' he complained, before issuing the further barb that he was 'sure that Lord Patel feels obliged to carry on with a crusade against the former staff, as to acknowledge his own errors would, no doubt, make his own position as chairman untenable'.

Gale may have been yesterday's man stomping off to plough different furrows, but his irritated outpouring took place as another prominent Yorkshireman, Michael Vaughan, found himself squarely in the firing line again. Vaughan had been another beneficiary of generous parole. Following Rafiq's accusation of the racist comment made to himself and other players in 2009 – the 'too many of you lot' moment that Vaughan has always maintained he neither remembers nor recognises – he was dropped from the BBC coverage of the disastrous Ashes series in the winter of 2021/22 – but then swiftly reinstated in March. When, in June, the ECB began the disciplinary investigation that Gale was to shun and which named Vaughan as a potential miscreant, the former England captain retained his place on the BBC team for the Headingley Test. This immediately prompted a letter of complaint from staff groups representing Black, Asian and minority ethnic workers at the company.

Vaughan took the immediate decision to step back from the situation. 'The key driver for this is my concern for the wellbeing of my family members and my wish to protect their family life,' he announced. He went on to talk of stepping back in the interests of the game and of minimising difficulties for work colleagues, having expressed regret about the way in which 'matters off the field take the focus away from what's happening on the field'. I think that ship's sailed, don't you, King Cnut?

I'd understand if the sons and daughters of York might be losing patience with me by now, but I'm going to ask them to stick with it. Your cricketing county, and those who represent it on the public stage as players and administrators, found themselves under the microscope and, to some extent, bore the sins of the world as they were roundly traduced. Those sins may have been real, but one can only hope that hundreds, if not tens of thousands, involved in the game at various levels, were not looking into their own souls and asking themselves whether they had questions of their own to answer.

By the summer of 2022, anybody with even the most tangential of interests in cricket could not have denied that the game needed to square up to issues about class and, of course, race. At the highest strata, in the English counties and at international level, it remained a largely, but not exclusively, white, middle-class pursuit. The ructions which followed the Rafiq affair – and I contend that this episode was very much the occasion, not the cause, of war – became particularly disturbing because the underlying implication seemed to this layer of people that they were being called racist. Institutionally racist. That's the term that everyone heard and to which almost all of them took great umbrage. And it is a term that is almost universally misunderstood in its slack application.

In April 1993, a Black teenager, Stephen Lawrence, was killed in a racist attack by a group of men in south-east London. The conduct of the Metropolitan Police in the months and years that followed has become a template for lazy, incompetent investigation, bred of entrenched attitudes and reinforced by deeply ingrained prejudice. In 1997, the Labour Home Secretary, Jack Straw, commissioned a report into the Met's procedures to be undertaken by retired high court judge, Sir William Macpherson. Two years later, Macpherson's report branded the force 'institutionally racist' and the term has been a part of public discourse ever since.

Its use is guaranteed to prompt anger, resentment and denial. It seems to suggest that anyone working in any industry, trade, occupation or profession labelled as 'institutionally racist' – a school, a legal practice, a police force, a cricket club – is, in fact, a racist. Macpherson's own words do not lead to any such conclusions. What he identified were 'processes, attitudes and behaviour which amount to discrimination through unwitting prejudice, ignorance, thoughtlessness and racist stereotyping which disadvantages minority ethnic people'. In other words, whatever an organisation's good intentions, as well as those of individuals working within it, if the outcomes resulted in clear patterns of disadvantage and inequality, then it was, in fact, institutionally racist. Those players, officials and a host of associated workers who would have had sleepless nights at the thought of being labelled a racist could have been better served by those whose careless use of the term had caused those individuals any grief or guilt.

Before anyone suggests that this is an over-liberal exoneration, it most definitely does not excuse anyone who thinks that 'elephant washer', 'waiter' or 'Paki' is 'just banter'. I have no idea whether or not Patel and his team have ever been fully briefed about the use of this potentially explosive term and neither do I know whether the ECB fully understands its use and application. It's an incendiary concept and the continuing coverage and comment about issues raised by Rafiq's case have hardly demonstrated a capacity for subtlety or nuance among those participating.

Other elements arising from the episode should have been more straightforward. What we might have been expected to be confident about would have been the use of accepted employment procedures by both the board and Yorkshire Cricket. In this, both parties demonstrated an impatience and inability to grasp detail that speaks ill of them. It is no excuse for them to argue that in this they were both operating at a time when senior politicians were blithely setting the tone for such laxity.

When judge Joanna Wade found that Andrew Gale and his colleagues had almost certainly been unfairly dismissed, she revealed that Yorkshire had failed to implement its own disciplinary code before handing him his P45. When the ECB brought charges of bringing the game into disrepute against 16 individuals in June 2022, it transpired that none of these individuals had been invited to a preliminary interview prior to this public accusation. The lowliest of trade union stewards would have recognised the utter clumsiness and untenability of such basic omissions on the part of an employer. Given that both the ECB and Yorkshire County Cricket Club are large organisations employing hundreds of people and operating under the public gaze, this cavalier, entitled approach speaks poorly of their operations. Obeying tiresome rules, wrestling with obstructive procedure, tackling tedious detail and showing willingness to engage with complexity. If those at the top of public British life couldn't be bothered with it, then you could argue that perhaps it's a bit much to ask some good chaps running the cricket to do so. But it hardly counts as an excuse in a grown-up world.

For all the clumsiness and ineptitude of both Yorkshire and the ECB when it came to the application of perfectly normal employment protocols, it would have been churlish not to acknowledge that there seemed to be a willingness within the game to accept some of its manifold shortcomings. It's not impossible to squeeze out sympathy for some at Yorkshire who could consider themselves marginally aggrieved that it had been their county alone that found itself in the eye of the storm. Patel, and those around him, for all their apparent impatience with those pesky old regulations, had, at least, acknowledged a problem. And the wind seemed to be blowing their way. Granted a temporary reprieve on their international ban, having seen two favourite sons win England a Test match at Headingley and basking in the good publicity of a well-staged event with a freebie thrown in at the end, any residual rumblings from Rafiq's revelations might, just might, blow over in time.

And just to bolster the feel-good factor, there were those Yorkshire boys again at the start of July, making their exploits against New Zealand look like yesterday's faded news. Conceding a first-innings lead of 132 to India – which would have been considerably greater had it not been for yet another resolute century from Jonny – England were set 377 to win in a day and a half at the Edgbaston Test. A purposeful start from Alex Lees and Zak Crawley seemed to have been squandered with the loss of three quick wickets. The usual jitters? The regulation collapse and surrender? Not with Baz's new England. Root and Bairstow, looking smooth and untroubled, biffed and glided along at just under five an over, ploughing their team smoothly towards a record-breaking victory again. The players, at least, were doing their best to offer distractions from the game's wider woes.

Over at the ECB, former international, Clare Connor, was in place as interim CEO. A new-look board of 11 people included five women and two people of colour. Mixed in with their collective expertise garnered from banks, accountancy houses, a smattering of public service and mid-range retail, all professed some love for, and knowledge of, the game. From umpiring in their local league, to holding office at a county club, to snaffling shares in the IPL, their profiles on the ECB website reveal strong ties to the game over which they now preside. On the back of the Rafiq-induced disruptions, they'd have known they had a job on their hands. And just in case they didn't, all they'd have needed to do was to peruse the impenetrable hieroglyphics that was English cricket's future fixture calendar.

So, sit tight – and pay close attention.

## Chapter 4

# The English cricketing calendar – a masterclass in fog and bafflement

*Confusion now hath made his masterpiece*

Macduff: *Macbeth*

WHEN IT comes to cricket broadcasting, there is a strong tradition dictating that some of the best entertainment comes in the gaps when rain stops play. Radio's *Test Match Special*, although noticeably attempting to throw off the mantle of clubability from the days of Blowers and CMJ, still caters to its committed audience with a tapestry of in-jokes and merry digressions. Yet, when it decides that it needs to, particularly with its choice of guests for scheduled intervals, it shows itself capable of analytical comment about the game and demonstrates a willingness to challenge its precepts and truisms.

Sky TV is fronted by commentary teams, most of whom are former international players, some of whom have shown themselves capable of perceptive, tough and critical comment. In common with their (sometimes interchangeable) BBC counterparts, they are somewhat hamstrung about what they can say. Snapping at the commercial hand that feeds you is never a good look. They know that sport at the highest level is now a commodity for TV: to believe otherwise is both fond and foolish. Given that this is the case, it's prudent for the ex-pro to do some lip-biting when the 'product' isn't always all that it's hyped up to be by the broadcaster's ads and publicity. But from time to time, they speak their mind to illuminating purpose.

It remains one of the characteristics of the British summer that just when you're about to settle in for an hour or two of TV cricket watching, the chosen venue will, even when it hasn't so much as drizzled in your area for a month, be afflicted by rain hosing mockingly from slate skies. Such was the scenario on 22 July 2022 when, with the four run-chasing Test dramas having given way to a slew of forgettable white ball games, England were due to play South Africa in what turned out to be a truncated 50-over game at Old Trafford. As the soppers and moppers went about their business in the background, Sky's principal commentators had much to ponder – and they set to it with varying degrees of intelligence and perceptiveness.

The most revealing comment, set among the blustering certainty of Ravi Shastri, the well-informed analysis of Eoin Morgan and the dull reticence of Shaun Pollock, came from former Test captain, Michael Atherton. His *Times* column and his observations on commentary mirror his batting; measured and thoughtful with the occasional waspish flourish. In a moment of professional candour, he admitted that although he was paid to comment on the game and enjoyed doing so, he was finding the fixture structure of the current season more than a touch baffling. Such confusion was, of course, a reflection of the overall domestic calendar that, as Atherton sadly conceded, had left even committed lovers of the game scratching their collective head. He had a point – and the grim numbers proved it for him.

Two days after Bairstow and Root had bowed out to a delirious Hollies Stand, having made light of an unprecedented run-chase, the circus came to town. Three T20 games against India were played over the next four days. At the completion of this 'series' and with a break of a further two days, three 50-over games were played against the same opposition over five days. No sooner had this set of games been completed than, two days later, three further 50-over games were played against South Africa over five days and ... wait for it ... two days after that, three T20s against them took place over four days.

Twelve international fixtures played over 24 days. And now I'm going to hazard a guess, the outcome of which can only ever remain speculative. I am going to suggest, assuming something about the readership of this book, which will be published some months after these games took place, that most of you would be able to recall with some confidence the results of the four Test matches played in June and July against New Zealand and India in the summer of 2022. I'm going to hazard a similarly confident guess that, among that same readership, your ability to recall the results of any of those 12 white-ball encounters will be significantly less perfect.

The argument here is not intended to be either sentimental or nostalgic. The plain fact is that cricket as a spectator sport now exists on varying levels. Among its players, governing bodies and – in England – its spectators, the accepted truism is that Test cricket is the game at its apogee. We'll be coming back to scrutinise that maxim later on. The 50-over game, so this perspective insists, is a decent halfway house in which players can hone skills that can look both ways. It can feed into the shorter, super-commercialised version and, increasingly, to the five-day game when occasion demands. The argument goes that shorter forms generate vital revenue and can be the hook for getting children interested in the game. Purists should just soak up the coloured monetisation of the game in the knowledge that it pays for higher culture while raw, ignorant but enthusiastic followers of their shorter form, with their lack of nuance and feeble attention spans, might get there in the end – and if they do, all well and good. By the end of July 2022, this rough-and-ready characterisation looked as shaky as it was one-dimensional – and one seminal event in particular gave Atherton, Morgan, Shastri and their colleagues ample food for thought on that damp Manchester day.

Four days earlier, Ben Stokes, newly installed as England's Test captain and the hero of the 2019 50-over World Cup win, announced that he would no longer be playing in that format for his country. His resignation followed that of Morgan three weeks earlier. The white-ball captain's personal form had been gradually slipping away and the final indignity of being unable to scratch a run in Holland, as England's batters filled their clogs in a pointless jolly, prompted him to step down. Stokes, whose own form had been skittish as he appeared to double-down on the mantra of unrelenting positivity, offered very different reasons.

'Three formats are just unsustainable for me now,' he tweeted. 'Not only do I feel that my body is letting me down because of the schedule and what is expected of us, but I also feel that I am taking the place of another player who can give the team their all.' In May, Stokes had called the workload 'unsustainable' for England players and talked of continuing to 'give his all' at Test and T20 levels. All of which started some hares running as the Sky team contemplated the state of the game.

If Stokes's resignation made headlines on the front and back pages, another cricketing event slithered quietly under the sporting news radar. On 13 July, Cricket South Africa (CSA) announced that it would be unable to fulfil its obligation to play three 50-over games in Australia in the coming winter. Given that their hosts, with tight schedules of their own to fulfil, were unwilling to shift the games, the ramifications for South Africa were significant. Lodged in 11th place in the world rankings, the Proteas were not guaranteed a place in the finals of the World Cup in India in 2023, where the top eight rated teams would participate. By failing to fulfil the Australian fixtures, crucial points towards qualification would be automatically conceded. It was a price CSA was prepared to pay.

It may well be that they had made a pragmatic judgement call. First, there was no guarantee of garnering points from the Aussies on their home territory, even though home advantage in ODIs at around 57% does not compare with Tests at around 72%. Second, they might just have looked at those around them in the rankings – Ireland, Sri Lanka and the Netherlands – and decided to back themselves to get through via the qualifiers in Zimbabwe in the summer of 2023. Or maybe, just maybe, and perish the thought, they thought that the ICC 50-over World Cup in India the following year was not that big a deal. Maybe they reckoned they had their own fish to fry and that they looked more appetising than a Malabar curry.

'As difficult as this decision has been for CSA,' explained its CEO, Phoeltsi Moseki, 'the long-term sustainability of our new T20 League is reliant on having all our domestic players available for this exciting new addition to the CSA calendar.' Moseki and his colleagues might have been looking at two things at once: their annual accounts and the international cricket schedule. And then, of course, sport does what it does best as South Africa's achievement of reaching the World Cup semi-finals in the autumn of 2023 seemed to suggest that it might all have been a bit of a fuss about nothing.

In the four years since the 2019 World Cup Final at Lord's, most of the major Test nations had played around 25 ODIs. New Zealand (10) and Pakistan (14) were outliers and, of course, Covid had played its part in disrupting proceedings. If the pandemic made it difficult to judge public appetite for the format, with restrictions as well as a degree of societal nervousness about attending any crowded event, an increasingly voiced suspicion was beginning to emerge that the 50-over ODI might be a format that was edging towards the end of its shelf life.

Of the 79 international games in the format played in 2021, more than a third featured non-Test-playing nations. England played six such games, all at home, winning three times against Pakistan and twice against Sri Lanka, with the remaining game rained off. Healthy crowds attended all the matches, with spectators stoically sporting fleeces in a chilly late-June affair in Chester-le-Street and boozily displaying beer bellies at rumbustious Edgbaston. Other than those five occasions, some 70 games were played around the post-pandemic world, often devoid of spectators. The distinct possibility, judging by reports and YouTube footage, is that the entire live audience for these remaining games probably equated to those in Durham who witnessed Joe Root smoothly rub out Sri Lanka's modest total in his sleep. Any TV coverage, as opposed to the online streaming platforms on which many in South Asia watch their cricket, would have, as ever, remained firmly behind the paywall.

The number of games increased in 2022, with 102 being played by the end of July. Of these, however, only 30 were contests between Test-playing nations. At the start of the year there were ten notional domestic 50-over leagues around the world – nine among the Test nations plus Nepal – none of which could be said to hold a prominent place in the fixture schedule. Even in established senior nations such as New Zealand, South Africa and Pakistan, leagues consisting of six-team competitions were shoehorned into the timetable. In many cases, regions and, increasingly, franchises do not select top-ranking players – a situation almost certain to occur because of the simultaneous staging of competitions as well, of course, as the strain placed on top performers by this crowded schedule. That, in itself, presents a marketing issue: if you've paid to see Stokes, Buttler and Rashid, there's a limit to how far their willing understudies can replicate their appeal.

In the English domestic game by 2022, the poor-relation status of the 50-over game became a de facto development. Michael Atherton's puzzlement during the rain break at Manchester is easy to understand once you steel yourself to decipher the cricketing calendar. I'm aware that what follows may not be news to many reading this, but it's worth charting the waters of cricket's offer to the English spectator both for the accuracy of record along with some wry amusement. The England and Wales Cricket Board

(ECB) invented their very own gordian knot. Hold tight while we try to unravel it.

At the start of April 2022, when cricket balls are rocks and winds can pierce three sweaters, the County Championship began. Players from outside England in the media often talk, with no great fondness, of their shock at being asked to perform in such conditions. The late Shane Warne once famously tweeted about playing in ten degrees and went on to observe that 'you lot have nine months of bad weather and three months of winter'. In 2022, a series of four-day games were played between these pewter days until the end of July. Interspersed with these contests, the 20-over Vitality Blast took place between the end of May and mid-July. There followed the usual bacchanalian jollity of Finals Day at Edgbaston, mercifully free of the chill of a September evening, with Hampshire running out winners. That's the easy bit.

On the second day of August the 50-over competition, the Royal London Cup (RLC), got under way. The next day, The Hundred started. Both tournaments had a full set of fixtures throughout the month, with the final of The Hundred scheduled for 3 September and that of the RLC for the 17th – nearly three weeks after the final qualifier. Most of the international stars of the short form of the game played in the lucrative Hundred franchise, meaning that the 50-over RLC was accordingly denuded of any glamorous pull, or even regular first-teamers in many instances. Meanwhile, there was the irritant of three Test matches which would hoover away players from the teams of England and South Africa who opted for white clothing and red balls. Just in case any young buck from the counties thought he might take the chance to impress the selectors with some hard-grafted four-day runs or hard-earned wickets, there were some red-ball county fixtures interspersed with the Blast between mid-June and the end of July for him to shine. Nobody managed to do so. His next chance would be on 5 September, with those games overlapping the Test matches against South Africa. They would then run on to the autumnal end of that month, interrupted only by the final stages of The Hundred and the RLC. When Sir Andrew Strauss, in his latest capacity as head of the ECB's high-performance review, conceded that the fixture calendar resembled a Rubik's Cube, he'd hit on a pretty accurate simile. We'll see how he got on with it later.

When referring to players, the paragraph above has been deliberately pronoun specific. In the midst of this stew of a schedule, England's women footballers provided a welcome moment of national joy by actually winning something and, in doing so, provided a sharp focus on the place of women's and girls' sport in society. Their achievements elbowed them to public notice and their conduct on and off the field of play endeared them to millions. Their cricketing counterparts were, no doubt, cheering them on from their sofas like the rest of us – but not, I suspect, without just the tiniest edge of resentment.

Meanwhile, just like their successful counterparts in another sport, rugby union, England's women cricketers had, for a couple of decades, been skipping around the men's game, jostling their fixtures around the 'real' schedule and often offered up as amusing support acts. There was a plus side to this. Having encountered these curtain-raisers, the cricket-watching public gradually recognised that women's cricket might be a different entity in many ways from the men's game, but that certainly didn't render it inferior. Among all the gushing recognition for the footballers, Heather Knight and her team could have been forgiven for being just a touch peeved at all the attention they were being afforded. They were, after all, World Cup winners themselves. But when it came to their own schedule, they could have been excused, like their male counterparts, for thinking that, to paraphrase the description of the bewildered American tourists of yesteryear, if it's Tuesday, it must be Northampton – or another non-Test county ground on which to showcase their talents.

England's women had started 2022 with a bumpy attempt at holding back the Aussie tide. Although they showed themselves to be made of sterner stuff than their male counterparts in that part of the southern hemisphere, their multi-faceted Ashes ended in defeat. In the World Cup in New Zealand in the spring, they emulated Eoin Morgan's men in 2019 by messing up a couple of winnable group games, thereby ensuring that they were, in effect, playing knockout cricket after just three matches. A nervy, one-wicket triumph over the hosts and a breeze against Pakistan saw them into the final against (yawn) Australia, where they were outplayed but not disgraced. In July, they steamrollered an indifferent South African side across the range of formats before heading off to Birmingham to win the gold medal in the Commonwealth Games that everyone wanted and expected. Except they didn't. Narrowly and unexpectedly beaten by India in the semi-final, they failed to pick up a consolation bronze when they were comprehensively dispensed with by New Zealand in the play-off. No need to tell you who won the gold.

With her reaction probably heightened by comparison to the footballers, veteran seamer Katherine Brunt told the media that 'it felt like the actual whole country was behind us – we're just sad that we let them down [and] couldn't quite do it'. But if one door was closing on women's cricket, another – for some, at least – was certainly opening. In the proper, time-honoured reaction to defeat of all professional athletes, Brunt was looking to the next game. 'I've got to get up in two days and play in The Hundred, which is savage – but that's just life, that's just sport.' She may possibly have been cheered by the knowledge that the hitherto accepted format of using the women's games as a pre-game taster was to be reversed in certain fixtures – an acknowledgement, perhaps, that cricket was taking baby-steps to equality of opportunity.

What she may have been less pleased by was the fact that the international side would have to wait until mid-September to meet again before they had the chance to exact some revenge on the Indian team that had beaten them to medal success. The Hundred may have afforded the game's big hitters, literally, a wider audience – and some of it, significantly, not hidden behind a paywall – but opportunities for the TV exposure so vital to growing the game for women and girls were becoming increasingly few. And that's worth digressing for a moment to consider.

In the days following the footballers' success, the commentariat was falling over itself to demand greater gender equality in PE lessons in schools. The players themselves wrote a joint letter to the two potential prime ministers, Rishi Sunak and Liz Truss, demanding that they 'make it a priority to invest in girls' football in school so that every girl has a chance' to succeed, proudly asserting that 'we see this only as the beginning'. It was a hugely laudable initiative and, given the promptness with which it was issued, must have been pretty well spontaneous. During the public celebrations that ensued, media coverage, quite correctly, sought out dozens of girls and young women almost overwhelmed with enthusiasm and joy at what their heroines had achieved. Goodness knows, I hope I'm proved entirely wrong, but I'm not brimming with the same optimism.

In Chapter 2 we looked at how overall provision in PE in state secondary schools for both boys and girls was being forced to fight its corner. The subject has been forced to battle against the waves created by the examination machine and funding cuts that make equipment, land and resources unattainable for all but the wealthiest, most of whom operate beyond the public sector. Much was made of Ian Wright's passionate rant that 'if girls aren't allowed to play football just like the boys ... in their PE after this tournament, then what are we doing?' England manager, Sarina Wiegman, who, as a youngster, had pretended to be a boy to be allowed to play, advocated junior school children playing together to normalise girls' participation. There's no denying the sincerity and passion of these remarks and the avalanche of similar comment from all quarters. The trouble was, as well intentioned as it was, this ardent advocacy of sport for all failed to realise that nobody, girls or boys, was getting enough of it in schools anyway. What's more, as mentioned earlier, if setting up kids to play football is relatively light on equipment and resources, cricket – even in its simplified forms – is a rather different matter.

The support structures and back-stories of the victorious Lionesses revealed a pattern of how they had been supported on their road to success. Along with interventions from schemes outside schools, some benefited from scholarships to private universities and eventually all were hoovered up by the giant corporation-type clubs from the more modest base of the football pyramid – who gained little financial benefit for having nurtured such talent. Among the tens of thousands of congratulatory tweets was one from Clare Connor, thanking the team 'for bringing it home – for showing girls that anything's possible'. There can be no doubting her obvious drive and sincerity in her tireless advocacy for providing girls with such opportunity: extending the reach of this opportunity beyond a very restricted field remains the challenge.

The composition of the England women's cricket squad, like that of the men's team, reveals a preponderance of ex-pupils from private and selective education. There are connections to sporting networks with top facilities and a number who have enjoyed some rather privileged and well-connected upbringings. The challenge – and there is no suggestion here that Connor, along with many others in cricket, is unaware of it – is to find talent and ability through wider participation and engagement with other strata of society. If mainstream media outlets during the height of 2022's scorched summer are anything to go by, reaching beyond cricket's known territory is a challenging business.

On a Saturday in late July, I settle down with a mid-morning coffee and my broadsheet newspaper of choice. I disentangle the sections and, in time-honoured fashion, dig out the sports section first. The Commonwealth Games has captured our attention and, unsurprisingly, there is significant coverage, particularly, of course, of any English (not British) success. Because of the forthcoming winter World Cup, the football season will be starting earlier than ever and so there is page after page of transfer rumour and profiles of managers and players in the Premier League. Rugby union is being played in the southern hemisphere and there is coverage of that, along with full cards and comment on the day's horse racing. There are a few random bits and bobs about tennis, rugby league and even chess and then, eventually, on one of the later inside pages, a brief round-up of yesterday's county cricket games along with the scorecards.

We're in high summer and cricket, in a newspaper whose coverage of the game is generally insightful and entertaining, has failed to attract more than a few column inches. Over the next few obsessive days, I monitor Sky Sports News. It's the same pattern: plenty of football, including scandalous behaviour by players with court cases involving them and their connections. Transfer news involving players from all corners of the globe proliferates and predictions are voiced from a platoon of sharply dressed, media-savvy pundits – although goodness only knows what any reliable analysis would reveal about the accuracy of their time-filling speculation. And even though Sky has access to much cricket footage, coverage of the game finds itself squeezed into the corners of the bulletins.

If I was merely playing around with this unsystematic dip into the invisibility of cricket, during the very weeks when it should have been at its most popular in England, someone else had been undertaking a more thorough – and pro-active – exercise. In July, Andrew 'Freddie' Flintoff headed up a three-part series on BBC entitled *Freddie Flintoff's Field of Dreams*. To those of us connected to the game – and those who had spent working lives dealing with truculent teenagers – none of it came as much of a surprise, as entertaining as it was. For many watching in its prime-time TV slot, it might have been a bit of an eye-opener.

Flintoff has built a media career on the back of his open and genuine good nature. These qualities, on top of his occasional heroics, are what lodge in the memory from a playing career in which, whisper who dare, the modest Test averages – batting at 32, bowling at 33 – utterly fail to tell the story of his achievements and appeal. He left his mark on popular consciousness, by coming up with the goods at crucial moments and, quite often, by the celebrations that followed. Having taken the final wicket in Mumbai to salvage a draw in a one-day series in India in 2002, Flintoff tore off his shirt and lassoed it around his head as he jubilantly careered away, revealing a torso that was more pie and chips than bench press and protein shake. At Edgbaston in 2005, he delivered an over of venomous fury against Australia, bowling Justin Langer and having two appeals for lbw against Ricky Ponting rejected before the Australian skipper nicked off to Geraint Jones behind the stumps. As Billy Bowden raised his crooked finger, Ponting put on the bravest face he could muster as he sullenly plodded from the colosseum of Flintoff's making.

In 2009 at the Oval, with his prowess all too obviously in decline and having recently announced his decision to retire from Test cricket, Flintoff magicked up one final gem of glorious unpredictability. With Australia chasing a notional 546 to win, Ponting (again) and Mike Hussey were building a solid enough foundation and at 217/2 could even have been harbouring faint, record-breaking notions of victory. When Hussey pushed for a tightish single to wide mid-on, he probably calculated that an increasingly inflexible Flintoff might just take a moment to stoop and collect, by which time both batters would be safely home. But there was nothing remotely arthritic about the fielder's swoop to the ball, the champion's nano-second of calmness with which he steadied himself and the ensuing missile of a throw that uprooted the stump at the end to which Ponting was, by now, desperately and futilely, running. In a now familiar response, Flintoff remained on the spot, beatifically threw his arms aloft and lifted his head to gaze to the heavens as his team-mates gleefully mobbed him. Such moments cemented his status as a national hero ... except that a decade or so later, kids from his home town of Preston didn't know who he was.

The premise of *Flintoff's Field of Dreams* is simple. Conscious of his own standing as one of the few players in the England team in which he starred who came from state schools, he embarks on a project to introduce the game to local teenagers, all boys. 'The fact is,' he explains, 'you either have to be lucky or privileged to play at the top level,' and that is what he's out to address. His establishment of this laudable ambition is followed by a shot of a group of three lads crouched over mobile phones, with one of their number, having located Flintoff's profile, haltingly reading out what he has discovered. 'Here he is ... international cricketer ... played for England ... never heard of him.' The action then cuts to Moss Side in Manchester where Flintoff locates an old mate, Nigel, who runs a boxing gym attracting a footfall of over 500 boys a week. The cricketer explains that this is the model he wants to adopt to introduce his own sport to the same sort of constituency. His mate pauses for just that second too long before wishing him well, without saying what is written all over his face: 'Well, good luck with that!'

During the following three hours of edited and slightly manipulated footage, Flintoff does, indeed, build a team of sorts, with the story finding a focal point in Adnan Miakhel, an unaccompanied child refugee from Afghanistan who demonstrates enough talent for Lancashire to pick him up for its academy once his asylum claim is eventually approved. With plenty of bumps in the road, Flintoff can express gratification that he has identified sufficient individuals who have been disabused of the fact that cricket, in the words of boxer Nigel, is not 'all posh, white and pavilions'.

In one telling episode, Flintoff starts an impromptu, rustic game on the grassed area at the centre of his old estate. His questions to various participants about whether they have ever seen a game of cricket – The Hundred perhaps – are met with polite but blank bemusement. 'Why would you come round here wanting to play cricket,' asks one young man – who turns out, eventually, to be one of the emergent team's stalwarts – 'when it's all football or rugby?' His query is not discourteous; just a plain and genuine statement born of bafflement.

In the maelstrom that was cricket's calendar in the summer of 2022, The Hundred was supposed to be the bearer of the game's hopes and dreams when it came to its intention to break free from its privileged enclave. Nestled in among three domestic tournaments criss-crossing each other with bewildering overlaps, along with Test matches and a slew of international short format games, this newest franchise occupied the prime August slots. For many of cricket's traditional followers, it was an unwanted cuckoo in the nest, but there were plenty involved at the top echelons of the game who were in no mood to be contemplating possible golden goose suicide. As the season drew to its autumnal close, one of those mandarins had his own little stir of the pot.

Chapter 5

# It's the economy, stupid. The poisoned chalice of Strauss's review

*O time! thou must untangle this, not I;*
*It is too hard a knot for me to untie!*

Viola: *Twelfth Night*

SEPTEMBER 2022 drew to a close with Ben Stokes's new England maintaining their cavalier ways with a series win against South Africa, although not before a stumbling, temporary return to old habits. Without ever quite obtaining the 29/3 landmark, a collapse from 81/3 to 149 all out at Lord's reminded us of what we'd been missing. After an initial defeat which slightly pricked the Bazball button, normal service was resumed with a thumping victory at Old Trafford and, eventually, another flawless run chase in a nervy low-scorer at the Oval.

Meanwhile, Surrey eased to the County Championship title, Hampshire won the T20 Blast, and Kent quietly took the second XI Royal London Cup at a half-full Trent Bridge, whose Rockets won the men's Hundred with the women's Oval Invincibles living up to their name. As the evenings drew in, England's shortest-form players started packing for Pakistan prior to yet another T20 World Cup (yes, there had been one the year before, in case you thought your memory was playing tricks with you) and the various princes of franchise cricket began to plan their global itineraries.

And beavering away in the background, Sir Andrew Strauss would have been putting the finishing touches to his High Performance Review (HPR) of men's cricket. Commissioned by the ECB after the limp surrender in the 2021/22 Ashes, the former England captain brought together an independent panel to take stock of the deterioration which afflicts England's red-ball cricketers once they board aeroplanes. In doing so, the panel took it upon themselves to inspect the structure and demands of the domestic game. 'We have heard loud and clear,' they concede, 'that the status quo in cricket is not serving the game – we play too much domestic cricket in an unbalanced schedule.' Of the 12-person panel, there were two women and two people of colour. Their report makes 17 recommendations aimed at sustaining the game's future and ensuring success for England across all formats. None of these touch upon how to extend the reach of the game or look at ways of connecting the game at grassroots level to its higher echelons.

Many of us have been the victims of the company's new brochure that plops uninvited on to our desks. It often takes a moment to grasp that the organisation being described is the one in which you spend your working life. Strauss's HPR is a sad parody of such publications. We have glossy snaps capturing sporting elation; differing font sizes and colour choices to attempt subtleties of mood and message; key ideas substantiated by stark, clear numbers – and everywhere, but everywhere, those harbingers of corporate dogma, the mission statements. 'We now require bold leadership' we are told, and the way to do it is to 'create high accountability' while we also 'foster a high-performance continuity'. Such vacuous nonsense probably informs everything from Shoreditch start-ups to oaths of loyalty to Xi Jinping. Strauss urges us to read the whole document 'as a holistic package' before seeking out the 17 recommendations and reacting to them as individual ideas. Whether many of those embedded in the counties and beyond took his advice is unknown. One thing was for sure: most of them – particularly those who don't host Test matches – didn't much like it.

In many respects, the good knight was never going to win – and there are some noble and proper aspirations expressed in the document. The expert panel itself may not have been a model of diversity, but it was able to acknowledge as a priority the need to 'do more to support and champion high potential individuals from all backgrounds who could become future leaders in cricket performance'. Moreover, given that his brief was to address shortcomings in the frail record of England's red-ball team, especially away from home, he knew that there was no way of avoiding collateral damage along the way – damage that would inevitably irk traditionalists. 'I am acutely aware of both the passion and strength of feeling around the domestic game,' Strauss informs us, but 'what is clear is that the current schedule is not optimal and must change.' The document ensures that the darkest and boldest font is employed to hammer home the point that 'the status quo is not an option'. And just in case us old duffers – for it is not a document aimed at iPhone scrollers with earbuds – hadn't quite been keeping up, it reminds us that 'with the proliferation of franchise T20 tournaments around the world [19 major tournaments are scheduled for 2024] the opportunities for talented young cricketers are significant'. How, he might have asked, are we going to keep them down on the Gloucestershire or Derbyshire farm, after they've seen Abu Dhabi?

In general, the HPR doesn't touch upon anything quite as vulgar as the acquisition of cold, hard cash. It confines itself to a recommendation that compensation mechanisms should be put in place to reward counties who develop young players who subsequently sign for rivals. Underpinning all recommendations is the central precept of developing a thriving domestic game with the ambition that 'England [will] be the world's best team across all formats within five years, for a sustained period of time.' Nowhere – and the authors would argue that it was not within their remit – does the document talk about cost and the financial implications for counties or the ECB. But for the sturdy yeomen and the few fair maidens of the shires, Strauss's report appeared to pose a threat to the very viability of their cricketing homes.

Despite his plea in the report to take an overarching view of his proposals, it was inevitable that the counties would make immediate, parochial calculations about what it meant for them. Their collective eye would have been drawn to the neat graphic on page 23 which laid out the grid of the domestic cricketing calendar starting from April in 2024 through to the following September. Those April weeks, with their potential for sleet or sunshine, are earmarked for a short, sharp one-day competition played in a single block 'when most white-ball players are available' and thereby strengthening match quality. From there, the County Championship would be played between May and July, interspersed with the T20 Blast in the two latter months.

August – which we'll revisit shortly – would principally remain dedicated to The Hundred, with the county game resuming throughout September. Kind of coherent … until you peer at the small print.

It's the County Championship, alright – just maybe not as we know it. The report proposes 'a top division of six to deliver best vs best' along with 'two second division conferences of six with one promotion place' to be 'played through the summer with a minimum of 10 matches per team'. Strauss would have known that he'd lit the blue touchpaper. Railing against this proposal, Kent issued an almost immediate condemnation, talking of 'the potentially irrevocable change to the essential nature of county cricket' before stubbornly asserting that 'we will not allow our Club to be rendered irrelevant'. Over at Essex, interim chairman, John Stephenson, was adamant that 'reducing the amount of red-ball cricket is not the way to produce better Test cricketers', and that his county 'would not vote in favour of any reduction in red-ball cricket' or in home T20s. Sussex chairman, Jon Filby, described Strauss's suggestions as 'unacceptable' and over at Surrey, Alec Stewart, the man whom Strauss replaced at the top of England's batting order, warned of alienating respected county members, who 'pay their money to come and support' providing the essential finance by doing so.

It might make for good knockabout fun to speculate on the aged, white and male nature of the memberships which these chairmen (all happy to be labelled in this gender-specific way) invoke. A stroll round any county ground on a Tuesday afternoon would do nothing other than reinforce this prejudice – as, of course, would the most cursory glance at the posh seats in stadia around the world referred to at the start of this book. To do so would be ever so slightly unfair. Conscious of attracting new audiences, particularly for white-ball games, many counties offer packages which bestow full membership, often with full voting rights for adults, at genuinely affordable rates. A scout around the websites of the counties reveals adult annual memberships for 2023 hovering around the £200 mark. Some come with voting rights along with priority booking for any other major games and all grant access to all county white- and red-ball cricket … with one immediate and startling exception. At those grounds where such games take place, if you want to watch The Hundred – the competition Strauss earmarks to take out the whole of August – in most cases, you'll have to cough up the extra.

It's worth taking a moment for reflection. It is unconscionable to believe that Strauss would not have anticipated the wrath of the counties. His loins must have been fully girded for that inevitable combat. But when he and his expert panel reaffirmed the dominance of The Hundred in its key spot for the whole of August, their decision was clear and unequivocal: 'The Hundred', the review asserts, 'is a premier white-ball competition and we believe its structure and prime-time schedule should be protected to retain this position.'

There was recognition that Test cricket needed to fiddle its way around the white-ball competition along with a proposal for a simultaneous 'festival' of red-ball cricket – a London Cup or a Roses Test. But in the prime holiday month for watching cricket, The Hundred was going to take pride of place. It's impossible to know the extent to which Strauss and his panel had factored in the attractiveness of this prized cricket product. As the leaves began to turn, did they suspect that by the time of the first frosts of a mild winter, the ECB would be in receipt of a bid of some £400m from private equity firm, Bridgepoint Group, for a 75% stake? Such a sum might well have caused eyes to water in an industry where journeymen pros on the county circuit do well to see £27k from a seven-month contract. But against the backdrop of the global cricketing stage, Bridgepoint's bid looked like meagre fayre.

Over at the offices of RP-Sanjiv Goenka Group (RPSG) in Kolkata, a smirk or two may have crossed their lips. In 2021, Goenka personally oversaw the purchase of Indian Premier League (IPL) franchise, Lucknow Super Giants, for a reported $950m. The *Times of India* quoted sources close to the entrepreneur of his determination to acquire an IPL team 'at any price'. Given that the US finance magazine *Forbes* estimates his net worth at around $2.3bn, it's hard to imagine that the purchase would have necessitated any belt-tightening in the Goenka household. What's more, it looks like it'll be an investment that could be feathering nests for some time to come.

*Forbes* estimates that each of the ten IPL franchises can expect annual growth in the region of 24%. With the average value of each franchise currently sitting at around $1bn, RPSG shareholders can expect better returns than those enjoyed by almost all US baseball and hockey teams. With growth rates of 10% and 16% respectively for the big money-spinners of NFL and basketball, the IPL is up there with global sport's economic elites. According to *The Athletic*, English Premier League teams who, in some cases at least, are bedevilled by the notion that their 'franchise' is dogged by the prospect of relegation from the elite, roll along at an average of 8% growth per season. And some of their number would grab your hand off for even that sort of return.

The tone and tenor of Strauss's document is informed throughout by the notion that Test cricket is worth preserving and that the pathway to success in that form of the men's game is through the traditional county system: a system that identifies and nurtures talent and which sees Tests, and playing for England, as 'the aspiration of our best young players' – an assertion substantiated by research done by the Professional Cricketers' Association. At the same time, the review recognises what even the most uncommitted follower of the game knows: the tide of the shortest forms of the game is galloping in. 'England', we are told, 'is increasingly competing with franchise leagues for talent, and therefore needs to have a central contracts system that is fit for purpose in the changing cricket world.'

Those of us who take an interest in sport are accustomed to applying sensible caveats when looking at the wages of elite performers. Life at the top is short and can be precarious. It's hardly the athlete's fault if wages reflect market worth: which of us would refuse a pay rise if offered? So, putting the gasping aside, let's do some sums – and for convenience of comparison, what follows is expressed in US dollars.

According to *The Cricketer* magazine, a full ECB annual red-ball contract can be worth up to $1m. In October 2022, there were 18 players on such contracts. Incremental contracts, of unspecified value, were awarded to six others, including, significantly, David Willey. Six fast bowlers of varying degrees of physical fragility were awarded developmental contracts – an acknowledgement of their potential and a useful way of ensuring priority of availability when required.

One year on, just as Buttler's men were finding new ways to underachieve during the 50-over World Cup in India, the ECB, in its boundless wisdom, deemed it the right time to issue its latest contractual updates. Once again, 18 players were awarded such central deals of whom only three, Harry Brook, Joe Root and the 33-year-old Mark Wood, were engaged for three years. There were two-year contracts for 15 others and eight players were kept for a single year, among whom the most notable inclusion was the increasingly creaking Ben Stokes. David Willey's reward for his loyalty in graciously accepting his fate when Jofra Archer was included in 2019 and his contribution in taking 11 wickets in the 2023 World Cup, second only to Adil Rashid, was to play on with some colleagues whose performances in the competition merited a stern word with themselves.

Contracted and non-contracted players alike receive match fees when playing for England: $15,000 for Test matches and $5,000 for white-ball appearances. Those who ply their trade at the higher levels of the franchise circuit augment these earnings significantly, with IPL wages offering the greatest largesse. Jos Buttler, Moeen Ali and Jofra Archer all enjoyed contracts in 2022 at around the $1m mark. Whether they looked across enviously at Virat Kohli pocketing double that amount is not documented, but they may well have raised an appreciative eyebrow at the $1.2m scooped by Liam Livingstone. Having made do with a modest $78,000 in 2021, a figure hardly repaid by his 42 runs in five innings for Rajasthan Royals, after a summer which saw him star in The Hundred, Punjab Kings opted to raise his wages 15-fold.

Mark Wood's fee of some $800,000 may look somewhat dim by comparison. The fast bowler always comes across as a particularly likeable chap and he would certainly have been devastated by the shoulder injury that kept him out of Lucknow Super Giants' team in 2022. Had he been available for all of their games, the maximum number of balls he would have bowled would have been 360, which comes in at just over $2,200 a delivery – although he'd cheerily remind you that he can give it a biff with the bat if required. The hum of white noise you can hear in the background is the battalion of wizened former quicks tutting and clucking about what their ability to churn through their routine toil of 20 over per day might have earned them in these more monetised times.

Strauss's brief was to try to untangle the mystery of the English domestic calendar and, just for the extra jeopardy, attempt to keep the county members happy at the same time. He concludes his remarks by expressing his view that 'we look forward to the game coming together and being bold in the face of a rapidly changing landscape'. That rapidity is embodied in the T20 leagues now established around the globe. Hold tight as we spin round the world to see where they are and when they play. And perhaps, before we do so, try to imagine yourself as a talented 16-year-old cricketer, male or female, and ask yourself what skills may serve you best as you survey the possibilities of the future.

All Test-playing nations host T20 franchises offering differing levels of reward and remuneration, with many holding contemporaneous women's competitions. In the last few weeks of 2022, England's men's team tied up a convincing series win in Karachi and the women duly walked through their T20 mismatch in the West Indies. The Caribbean men's team fared dreadfully in Australia and probably sprinted back to the airport. Some of the participants in those games might well have been looking at the next few months and sizing up where and when they could next exercise their skills for more recognition and greater remuneration. The Lanka Premier League – benefitting from ambassadorial roles for Sanath Jayasuriya, Wasim Akram and Viv Richards – had already run its anonymous course, resulting in victory for Jaffna Kings. With total prize money for the winning team weighing in at a paltry $100,000, it attracted no overseas starlight – unless you count the ever-willing Ravi Bopara – to force it into general notice.

Almost as it finished, in New Zealand, the Super Smash began, continuing until the following February, overlapping both the Big Bash in Australia and the Bangladesh Premier League. Down in South Africa, the SAT20 began in mid-January 2023 and ran its course until the start of February when the Pakistan Super League soaked up any basher, tweaker or dasher who hadn't acquired the golden ticket for the gravy train of the IPL, starting in late March and finishing in late May. Back in England, old pros and young hopefuls began plodding circuits of the outfield while dreading slip practice in the fog and frost. For those who hadn't made it to the major – or majorish in some cases – platforms, there might come opportunities anew with the Caribbean Premier League, due to start at the end of August.

If these competitions are now becoming firmly fixed in the international calendar, there are still plenty of others floating around in the imaginations and boardrooms of the cricket world. Some have genuine promise and others are pedalling furiously in the hope of being caught in the slipstream of the T20 gold rush. The Euro T20 Slam, involving teams from Ireland, Scotland and the Netherlands, along with the UAE's International League have yet to flower, despite attracting big names – Kieron

Pollard, Moeen Ali, Phil Simmons, Paul Farbrace –
on to potential playing and coaching staffs. There are
competitions in Nepal and Kenya and plenty of talk of a
new Saudi T20 competition drenched with sportswashed
dollars. And then there's the introduction of Major League
Cricket in the USA.

'We believe for American fans this is the stereotypical
perfect game – three hours long, extremely exciting,' co-
founder Sameer Mehta told *Forbes* magazine. The six-team
league launched in July 2023 with plenty of big names
from the circuit, of whom, parochially, the most prominent
was Jason Roy. Money will not be a problem. Meeha,
along with his brother Sudir, have an estimated net worth
of $6.4bn, acquired principally from the Torrent Group,
a company involved with pharmaceuticals and providing
power supply. He sees a window to develop the game in the
US, particularly in those areas where significant numbers of
people of South Asian heritage reside, during the relatively
quiet US sporting months of June and July. The dates are
carefully chosen to ensure that there is no competition from
other T20 franchises. He acknowledges that Test cricket
may be being played in England at the time but does not
regard that as an obstacle. He tells *Forbes* that he is certain
of the appeal of the US to top cricketers and of how Steve
Smith has personally told him that it is a possibility that he
is 'keen to explore'.

There is, of course, every possibility that Sameer Mehta
could be the new Allen Stanford – with the obvious exception
that he does, in fact, seem to have some real money. That is
not the point at issue. What's important to understand here
is that owning and promoting franchise cricket is seen not
just as a potential goldmine. Association with a star-studded

confection, labelled with a vague geographical identity, is a glowing status symbol for those who see the acquisition of a sporting franchise as a way to confirm their own value, standing and respectability way beyond the world of mere sport. Cricket may not be operating on the sportswashing scale of those who acquire Premier League football clubs or manipulate the award of major tournaments to their own back yard. And on another level, one probably should applaud any evangelising effort to take the beautiful game to different lands. But one thing is for certain. Any irate, perplexed county chairman who thinks he's performing in the same circus as the likes of Sameer Metha, needs to have a very stern word with himself – and, yes, this time I'm being very gender-specific.

It's important to avoid clichéd views here. There is no suggestion that all county boardrooms are full of fusty old colonels waiting for tiffin and scratching their heads in bewilderment at how those fellows from the colonies seem to have become so damned good at our game. There is ample evidence of forward thinking and there is plenty of good work being done to connect with communities and to tap wells of talent that could grow the game both locally and nationally – and we'll look at some outstanding examples later in this book. The problem here, and I don't wish to become too metaphysical, lies with conceptions of what different people imagine the game to be. I'll give you my best shot at explaining what I mean.

Cricket from bygone eras looks and feels like an entirely different animal from its current counterpart. Take, as a starting point, WG Grace. History tells us that he was the foremost cricketer of his generation. The stats available to us, albeit there is some suggestion that these are not the most watertight of records, renders this an uncontroversial statement. To go with these, there exists some limited footage of him giving a batting demonstration to an admiring audience. Even allowing for the creakiness of the filming technique, WG displays a disappointingly inelegant and alarmingly static method, relying, as far as we can discern, on a good eye and some beefy forearms which he uses to clip away with a bat that might just do service for a decent game of beach cricket. Grainy, jerky film places him, immovably, in a different era. But what about those stats?

Leaving aside the remarkable fact that he played at the highest level for some 44 seasons, his achievements are astonishing. One of his best seasons was in 1876 when, at the age of 28, he scored 2,622 runs and took 129 wickets. The trouble is – and I'm not doubting his obvious ability – it just doesn't ring true to me: daft old sods, girths overhanging their flannels, standing still with no footwork and bashing away at half-trackers delivered by arthritic trundlers. It just looks so hopelessly slow and lacking in energy, doesn't it? It's not real cricket at all.

Grace had many wonder years if figures are to be believed, but, for convenience, let's take the runs and wickets of 1876 as a point of reference. He achieved this 77 years before I was born and about 86 years before I embarked on my lifelong fixation with the game. For any similarly afflicted nine-year-old in 2022, 86 years takes us to 1946. What does the game from that era, as seen on film, look like? From the evidence available, I would strongly suggest that what's revealed is a world that begins to bear some distant familiarity and connection to someone in, for example, their sixties or seventies in 2022. For the nine-year-old, however, what is on offer is a world as alien, peculiar and even cartoonish as the inflexible Doctor Grace flapping his toy bat around.

One particular piece of film from around that time opens an entertaining window into ancient history for our nine-year-old. A British Council production of 1948, it adopts a genially informative, if schoolmasterly, tone as it looks at cricket, taking as its focus the Lord's Test against Australia. Narrated by Sir Ralph Richardson and John Arlott, an opening caption explains that 'the purpose of this film is not to teach cricket to the unbeliever, but to give pleasure to the converted' – a maxim that could, perhaps, stand for some of the stultifying attitudes that bedevil cricket nearly eight full decades later. Arlott talks us through the ritual of pitch preparation before footage of decorous crowds in jackets and hats – although later in the day revealed in shirt-sleeve order – merrily file out of St John's Wood station and start to snake around the recognisable brick perimeter wall of the ground. It's not yet what you'd call a stadium.

The recording of the game itself has become more fluent since Grace's day, although somewhat hit-and-miss in its ability to capture key moments. What is immediately evident, however, is a briskness and lack of histrionics in any of the action. Bare-headed batsmen are dismissed and walk off without demur; there's certainly no send-off from the bowler who might, just might, receive a pat on the back from a colleague. No fielder even contemplates putting the dive in around the boundary, opting instead for a half-hearted poke with a boot as the ball passes him by. Umpires in long white coats preside over matters as bowlers go smartly about their business, the record showing that they bowl 550 overs in five days' play. Set 404 to win on the final day, the visitors achieve this for the loss of three wickets with the hosts accommodatingly bowling 114 overs to allow them to do so. The star of the show is the WG Grace of his era, Donald Bradman, who scores an unbeaten 173. The crowd, nestling on the advert-free boundary rope, remain to the end to sportingly applaud this feat. The game was undoubtedly fiercely and seriously contested, but to modern eyes, proceedings look distinctly antiquated and quaint. Our nine-year-old struggles to see connections with cricket in 2023.

But surely, Bradman, with his Test average of 99.94 and his place in the game's pantheon of fame, is somehow bound to our 21st-century nine-year-old? Possibly. He played in 52 Tests, 33 of which were on home turf and 37 of which were against England. He scored 6,996 runs in 80 innings, placing him 56th in the list of all-time Test run-scorers. In contrast, Sachin Tendulkar played 200 Test matches around the world scoring 15,921 runs during a bruising schedule at an average of 53.78. Bradman's countryman, Ricky Ponting, played 168 Tests, scoring 13,378 at 51.85 and topped that off with 375 one-day international appearances. Closer to the heart of the modern game, now beating in India not Lord's, the princely poster boy, Virat Kohli, chips in with 111 Tests (8,676 at 49.29) along with 265 ODIs and 115 T20 internationals – and a net worth of around $125m.

Cricket in 2023 is seen by different constituencies through a variety of lenses and for a variety of purposes and with a variety of expectations. These may be influenced by age, geographical location, a sense – or not – of historical perspective and the place of the game in a nation's or a region's sporting preferences. Strauss, charged with addressing some of the perceived ills of the English game, found himself trying to repaint a small corner of a panoramic landscape – and one corner of that panorama, guarded by the stalwarts of the counties, probably wasn't going to be happy with whatever he did. And what's more, as events unfolded for England's cricketers from the autumn and winter of 2022 up to the classic Ashes series of 2023, he could have been excused for asking himself whether he'd been asked to fix something that wasn't so badly broken after all. And he'd have known for certain that the Rafiq affair definitely hadn't faded into oblivion either.

## Chapter 6

# If it's 2022, it must be a World Cup. Somewhere

*Things done well and with a care, exempt themselves from fear*

Henry VIII: *Henry VIII*

THE COVID pandemic that hit the world in March 2020 was not a good thing: but there were redeeming features. It allowed humanity to demonstrate its capacity to cooperate in order to enhance scientific and medical expertise. It enabled experts to deploy knowledge and ingenuity with speed and creativity.

It bought the best out of armies of volunteers and reminded us, however temporarily, that those who earn their wages doing the most apparently menial of tasks are, in fact, among society's most valuable assets. All of which is just as well, because in a parallel universe, blowhard politicians awarded dodgy contracts to their venal mates and narcissistic has-beens puffed themselves up on Instagram and Twitter by spewing bilious pseudo-science, while the vulnerable died in their tens of thousands. But even worse, Covid played absolute havoc with the sporting calendar.

In the summer of 2022, England's triumphant women footballers captured first the attention, and then the hearts and admiration, of the sporting public. Their tournament had been postponed from 2021 and, in this respect, it was the first of a number of such delayed events. In October and November, rugby league staged its rescheduled premier global competition in England, claiming, with some justification, to be breaking new ground in terms of inclusivity and sustainability. While England's men contrived to lose to Samoa in the semi-finals, having obliterated them 60-6 in the group stages, the women failed valiantly at the same stage against New Zealand who, in turn, were squashed by the Australian steamroller in the final. But it was the wheelchair game that managed to print itself on the imagination of newcomers to a game broadcast free-to-air on the BBC. On top of the live attendance of 4,500 at Manchester Central, some 1.3 million viewers tuned in to witness England's bone-cruncher of a victory over France, every single one of us wincing and grimacing our way through the entire spectacle.

On 12 November in New Zealand, the same day that the rugby league men's team lost to Samoa, England's women's rugby union team had conformed to expectations and extended an unbeaten run to 30 games by reaching the World Cup Final. In another tournament delayed by a year, this record was undone by the hosts who completed a last-gasp victory, having been behind for most of the game. England's Lydia Thompson had given them a reluctant helping hand by being sent off after 17 minutes with her team leading 14-0.

In a few weeks of brushes with potential success, rugby in its various manifestations had provided sparkling shows and had dallied with triumph, but it was only the iron men in wheelchairs who finished with a pot to put in the cupboard. With ITV holding the rights for the union games, all matches in both codes had been free to air. On the same platforms later in the month, England's footballers flattered to deceive in Qatar, with some of the usual flirtation with success along the way. Meanwhile, stubbornly behind the paywall, England's men's cricketers embarked on a World Cup of their own.

Covid, of course, played tricks with our perceptions of time in a host of ways. It might have been that there were those in the cricket-watching public who could have sworn there had been a World Cup just a year ago. And they'd have been right, of course. The 2020 event, scheduled for Australia, was eventually played out in the cavernous echo-chamber of sterile stadia in Oman and the UAE in the autumn of 2021. Of the 32 games played once the Super 12s had been established, conditions in the desert played the most influential hand in the outcomes. Of sides batting second, 22 were victorious. In the ten instances where those batting first prevailed, only four of these games were between Test-playing nations; in the remaining fixtures, the senior nation was always the winner. None of which could have accounted for 15 minutes of madness in Abu Dhabi where, even by English sport's fine record of manufacturing unnecessary disappointment, a new depth was drilled.

In the semi-final, requiring 57 from 24 balls, New Zealand's Jimmy Neesham lashed a quick 27 off 11 balls of varied filth from Chrises Woakes and Jordan. Meanwhile, Daryl Mitchell belted four sixes at the other end to get to the target with an over to spare. With weary inevitability, Australia went on to win the final. Two weeks earlier,

England had contemptuously knocked off the 125 needed to beat them in the group stages, needing fewer than 12 overs to do so. The ambition of adding the T20 trophy to the World Cup and thus establishing themselves as undisputed white-ball champions had been thwarted – but at least another global competition was only just around the corner to put things right.

In May 2022, Matthew Mott was appointed head coach of England's white-ball team. Mott, whether anyone other than Eoin Morgan himself knew it or not, would soon be working with a new captain, Jos Buttler, as well as a new team. With the appointment of McCullum to the leadership of the red-ball team and Rob Key's tenure as managing director of England men's cricket only a few months old, gusty changes were blowing through England's men's set-up.

For Mott, selected on the back of his success in the women's game in Australia, the brief could not have been clearer: only trophies would do. Given that he was selected for his coaching prowess and not his media skills, he should be forgiven for tolerating the release of comments that could have been generated by statement-bank: '… fully aware that this team has been functioning well … initial plan to work with the playing group … maintain, then enhance success …' Such corpo drivel has become the stock-in-trade of all major sporting bodies. Key himself referenced Mott's 'varied coaching journey' (you're nobody unless you've been on a journey) and of 'being aligned with what we want to do.' Of insider, Paul Collingwood, who had failed in his bid for the job, Key talked of how he would remain 'an asset in our environment'. Once Mott had walked his unnecessarily full-strength side through three daft games in Amsterdam – an event, one suspects, jointly commissioned by the post-Covid

Dutch tourist and brewing industries – the unerring focus had to be on the 2022 World Cup in Australia in the autumn.

England went to the tournament as second-favourites behind Australia, with India, depending on your choice of bookmaker, either close behind in third or pipping them into second place. Injuries to key players Jasprit Bumrah and Ravindra Jadeja had blown a hole in their preparations with an effect on the composition of their team more drastic than Jonny Bairstow's daft golfing accident at the beginning of September. Given the freakish nature and timing of the injury, he could have been forgiven the clichéd 'gutted' response on his Twitter account. His potential replacement, however, was to pose an ethical, as well as a managerial, problem to brave new England.

The stand-and-deliver form of Jason Roy had been steadily deserting him in both 20- and 50-over cricket. There were potential contenders around the scene, one of whom, Phil Salt, had shown skill and ability during the English summer and went on to acquit himself admirably in the mini-marathon series in Pakistan, which we'll deal with in the following chapter. But in the world of gun-for-hire batters in global franchise cricket, there was an English long-legged elephant in the room: Alexander Daniel Hales.

In ten years of brave, often elegant batting, from Mumbai Indians to Sydney Thunder to Karachi Kings to Trent Rockets, with various points in between, Hales has scored just shy of 13,000 T20 runs in nearly 500 games, 75 of which have been at international level. He has an average of around 30, reaching 50 or more on around one occasion in six and with an overall strike rate hovering around 135. That he has/had, like so many people of his generation, a liking for recreational drug use, seemed to have brought an end to his international career.

In April 2019, three months before the 50-over World Cup in which he was expected to feature, Hales failed a routine test for the use of recreational drugs – the second time he had done so. Already under a degree of public scrutiny for his aggressively passive involvement with Stokes's Bristol fracas in 2017, the batter did not seem to be a quick learner. 'It was … an eye-opener to how much we are in the public eye as England cricketers,' he had told the *Guardian* about the brawl. 'You have to mature and put yourself in the right situations, not be out at 2.30am in the middle of a series.'

None of which stopped him from doing what would have been an everyday dalliance with mildly mind-altering substances – possibly excusable youthful exuberance, had he not been an international sportsman. ECB regulations stipulated that it was only after a second offence that the board needed to be informed of such misconduct. Any crunch would come after a third violation, which could end with the termination of a contract. Subsequent reports suggest that whatever the letter of the protocols demanded, Morgan, Hales's international captain, was first apprised of just such a violation when he picked up his daily paper. He was not a happy man, albeit his ire was directed firmly at the player rather than the administrators who had been stunned into dumb paralysis by the affair.

'We've worked extremely hard on our culture in the last 18 months since the Bristol incident,' a visibly frustrated Morgan told the assembled media, going on to acknowledge the team's recognition of their duties as role models. 'Unfortunately, Alex's actions have shown complete disregard for those values … This has created a lack of trust between

Alex and the team.' His comments followed a meeting between himself and five senior players – Buttler, Moeen, Root, Stokes and Woakes – and although this impromptu body had no executive powers, the ECB, in the persons of Ashley Giles and Tom Harrison, endorsed this decision. As it turned out, Hales was not missed at the top of the order as a joyous Roy in his muscular pomp got England off to a series of racing starts along with the pre-golf Bairstow. Ethics and morality seemed to have trumped sporting necessity – and the gods seemed to have been on the side of the righteous. He had not turned out to be indispensable.

The reaction to his recall in September 2022 to the England squad for the Pakistan series prompted some interesting analysis. Any recorded comment from Morgan in response to pundits eager for clips and clickbait confined itself solely to Hales's batting prowess: 'There's no doubt he's extremely destructive and a match-winner,' he told Nasser Hussain on Sky in August. His subsequent selection was greeted with silence by Morgan, who notably failed to contribute to a post-match interview with the player following the team's victory over Sri Lanka which saw England into the semi-final.

Hales's team-mates were equally limited in the scope of their comments, referring only to the process of their decision-making, not the content of their deliberations. 'I spoke to lots of the senior players to make sure no one would have any issues with Alex being back in the team if we wanted to select him,' Buttler told *The Cricketer* magazine. 'No one had any issues,' he added, pointing to the player's 'excellent form' and of his experience since he last played for England. The new captain declared himself pleased with the process, which he compared with Morgan's handling of the situation in 2019, giving 'ownership to other guys'. Except, of course, he wasn't exactly comparing like with like. Morgan had insisted on dropping Hales, notwithstanding his form and ability, because of his conduct. Buttler and his team's rationale seemed to rest entirely on Hales's merit as a player. Readers will be unsurprised to know that the ECB remained resolutely non-committal during the whole business.

Having acquitted himself adequately, but not as well as Ben Duckett or Phil Salt, in the Pakistan T20 series, Hales had his place in the 15-man squad for Australia confirmed. These 15 men were a reasonable reflection of the nation they were representing. With two English-born players of Pakistani heritage and two other Black Britons, as well as the Test captain with parental links to New Zealand and a plethora of those with origins from South Africa and other parts of the world, the white-ball team was, as it had been for some time, significantly more diverse than most of its Test-playing counterpart. In 2019, comedy politician, Jacob Rees-Mogg, achieved the seemingly impossible by showing himself to be even more dense than we had thought possible by observing that the World Cup victory clearly demonstrated that 'we don't need the EU to win'. If he'd had any measure of self-awareness (yes, yes) Rees-Mogg, a keen supporter of Somerset cricket, might have been watching from behind his chaise longue as England's mixed band of brothers went about redeeming the previous year's slip-up in the Emirates.

Before they even took to the field, however, the game had witnessed a shift in its tectonic plates. Eight sides who had not qualified automatically for the latter stages needed to slug it out for the chance to play big-boy cricket. In Group A, Sri Lanka had to suffer the indignity of navigating their way past the Netherlands, Namibia and the UAE – a feat they managed with relative comfort after the shock of defeat to the African nation in the opening game. Down in Hobart, all Group B games were played in front of crowds that never reached the 3,000 mark. While not exactly the mandatory group of death required by any tournament, the bringing together of Scotland, Ireland, Zimbabwe and the West Indies conformed to the other sporting cliché of there being no easy games at this level.

In 2021, T20 World Cup holders, West Indies, although having pre-qualified for the latter stages, managed just one victory – a three-run win over Bangladesh in Sharjah – in their five group matches. If the raucous memory of Carlos Brathwaite's delirious team-mates rushing across the outfield at Eden Gardens in Kolkata in 2017 had evaporated by then, things were about to get a whole lot worse. After limp surrender to Scotland in their opening game, the situation was retrieved by victory against Zimbabwe, leaving the nation that had once been the most feared and respected across the game needing to beat Ireland to qualify. By the time chunky Paul Stirling beamed his way back to the pavilion, having guided his side past the target of 147 with just one wicket down, for those of us of a certain generation, a new world order had been confirmed. Stirling's men, of course, were far from done with their contribution to the tournament.

Although local conditions didn't play as significant a part as they had done in the desert the previous year, a damp Australian spring made its mark on the tournament throughout. One of the consequences of this was that there were to be no flat tracks giving licence to the musclemen batters to set up games of 210 plays 200. Three games were washed out entirely – a fate which seemed to threaten the final itself, only for the weather gods to defy expectation by instructing storm clouds to encircle the MCG but to allow a full game to take place. Sides batting first in the tournament were marginally more successful, winning on 16 occasions as opposed to 13 by those chasing. Of those 16, three were determined by the masonic Duckworth-Lewis-Stern method – and of these, the most significant for England and their followers was in Melbourne on 26 October.

One of the central precepts informing the narrative of this book is that England's cricket authorities seem to get more things wrong than right. All the same, I'd venture to suggest that had they witnessed a crowd of just over 11,000 people for a World Cup group game in a stadium capable of housing nearly ten times that many, even their most obtuse member would have recognised that something had gone awry. Over 90,000 had been present three days earlier to see India edge past Pakistan and the organisers' ploy of playing double headers ensured that grounds where both of these teams played brought respectable attendances.

But other games were less attractive to the Aussie paying public. The dismal weather probably played a further part in keeping people away on the soggy Wednesday of the Anglo-Irish derby. Once that game came to its early end, it rained in Melbourne for 48 hours, washing out the subsequent three games, including two of Afghanistan's scheduled fixtures and England's prime meeting with the home nation. Although Ireland were unable to play a potentially influential fixture against the Afghans, their joy at once again having seen off a tentative England in a major competition – they had triumphed in a heady run chase in Bengaluru in the 50-over competition in 2011 – provided delirious compensation.

Baz, of course, was not part of the set-up as England went about their business in Australia. Had he been, he may have been discomfited by a team apparently caught between rhetoric and pragmatism. Eoin Morgan's leadership and the success it engendered had been built on the fierce mantra of refusing to be cowed by fear. Much of the time, particularly when it came to the team's batting, this was – and continues to be – characterised by a determination to attack, irrespective of the loss of wickets. The rationale is clear: occasional failure is inevitable, but success will outweigh failure over time. When faced with knocking off 113 to beat Afghanistan in their opening game in Perth, the swashbucklers appeared strangely inhibited and although the match was won with low-key commonsense, it was not before some of the main batters, to use a term banned, no doubt, in that den of positivity that is the England dressing room, threw their wickets away.

Four days later at a dank MCG, Buttler invited Ireland to bat and, with solid contributions from Balbirnie and Tucker, they posted a respectable, but not daunting 157. And then, when England went in to bat, it happened. Time to WhatsApp – and this time I'm the first one there. With the first ball of the fifth over, his first of the game, Fionn Hand nipped one back off the pitch to bowl Stokes between bat and pad. 29/3. With England's strokemakers stifled by a combination of tight bowling, long boundaries square of the wicket and, once again, an apparent lack of belief in the go-hard commitment, the target began to look more challenging by the minute. And the rain was approaching. And the Duckworth-Lewis-Stern target was becoming a more ominous warning light on the scoreboard with every passing over.

When Malan's scratchy stay came to a merciful end, dismissed off the first ball of the 13th over, the score was 86/5. Livingstone joined Moeen knowing that they needed to get a shift on to avoid an embarrassing defeat. He popped a single down to long on and in the subsequent eight balls, Moeen rattled up 19 runs. Just two more decent shots in the three remaining balls of Gareth Delaney's over and England would be ahead of the game and normality would be restored. Umpires Paul Reiffel and Adrian Holdstock, however, judged that playing conditions had deteriorated to the extent that even reaching the end of the over was not a possibility. Rain stopped play in Melbourne – and did so for the next three days.

'I've seen a lot of rain in my time playing cricket and I've never been happier to see that rain come down,' said Balbirnie, the Ireland captain. For England, the breathing space that should have been afforded by playing two lesser nations in their opening games had been carelessly wasted. When the clouds loured and spouted over the MCG two days later, washing out their game against Australia – one of the tournament marquee moments – they were back to where they had been in 2019 after defeat to Sri Lanka. From now on, it was knockout cricket.

With the abandonment of the Australia game, England's captain expressed clear regret. 'It's one of the biggest games of your career,' said Buttler, 'so we're disappointed not to be able to play … our focus is now on our next match to keep our tournament alive.' An initial reaction might also have been to express some sympathy with Cricket Australia (CA), the organisers of the competition. According to the Australian Government Bureau of Meteorology, October 2022 saw 142mm of rain in the Melbourne area compared to the average 66 – although not such a huge increase on the 110 of the previous year. This had also brought with it slightly cooler temperatures than usual, a factor probably instrumental in deterring attendance. But any slack cut for CA would be unnecessarily generous.

October in Victoria may not quite be Derbyshire in April, but summer is certainly not in full bloom. On 24 September, the MCG had been packed to the rafters as 100,024 people watched Geelong beat Sydney Swans to win the Aussie Rules football Grand Final. Cricket, like its lake spring equivalent in England, was just feeling its way into the season. Way out west in Perth and over in Adelaide, monthly temperatures were rising to the low 20s and rainfall might be expected to be lower than that in Melbourne – 40mm and 50mm respectively. Over in Brisbane it'd be warmer, but maybe wetter, and Sydney's numbers differed little from Melbourne. Of the seven scheduled for Melbourne, three were washed away on top of England's DLS game with Ireland. Only one other fixture, Zimbabwe's clash with South Africa at Hobart – average temperature 17 degrees and 40mm rainfall – was lost to weather.

Back in 2014, CA had agreed the hosting of the competition with the ICC and earmarked the months of October and November. There would be no Ashes or any other major Test series to cloud the issue and, besides, CA now had a gleaming new asset, in the form of the Big Bash, to protect. The best way of doing so was to keep it in its prime place during high summer. This self-interest was no different from any other of the major playing nations in terms of giving priority to their main income generators. But with no reserve days in place other than for the final, CA might just have been a little quicker on its feet – especially if it were to insist on Melbourne, and the MCG in particular, playing host to many of the prime matches in October and November.

Five kilometres from the MCG sits the magnificent Marvel Stadium. When I describe it as such, all I have to go on is its gleaming website. While I've spent a few days at the G (including one particularly chilly December day, as it happens) I've not been to the Marvel, so I'm taking the site designers at their word. Were I to live in the city, however, there's every chance that I'd have had first-hand experience of it. It has staged musical acts from Eminem to Taylor Swift to Ed Sheeran to the Foo Fighters. There have been international rugby union tests, football World Cup qualifiers and USA basketball action. Domestically, it offers AFL, A-League (football) and plenty of cricket in the Big Bash, where it is home to the Melbourne Renegades. It has a capacity of just over 53,000 and, just one more thing: it has a roof. On only two occasions during the tournament did attendances exceed the Marvel's capacity – India's game with Pakistan and then the final – both at the MCG. Australia's opener against New Zealand in Sydney was well below capacity at 34,000. To be constantly threatened by weather, given the availability of a neighbouring stadium equipped to pre-empt its worst effects, seemed to be a sloppy dereliction of duty by those entrusted with staging a global event. And if CA needed their noses rubbing in it, their clumsiness was given one final airing just three days after the final in which the home team had never come close to featuring.

Perhaps the three 50-over ODIs between Australia and England, played over five days at three different venues just four days after the final, had been planned as some sort of sadistic, gladiatorial march of the victors. Whether a home victory might have brought the citizenry out in gloating triumph is impossible to know. What is more certain is the utter indifference displayed by the cricket-watching public towards an almost meaningless bilateral series. The 15,000 who turned up at Adelaide was marginally trumped by the 16,000 at Sydney two days later. By the time it was back to the G three days after that with Australia 2-0 up, even these figures seemed healthy compared to the 10,000 who were in Melbourne – although there is plenty of ocular proof to suggest that this official figure may have been on the generous side.

The home side completed a whitewash victory and moved into fourth place in the international one-day rankings while England dropped to second. If that represented some sort of consolation for the players and their board, any bombast from the usually brash Australian media was notably absent, even after Jos Buttler's dismissive snipe about being 'not fussed at all' about the defeat. 'Any time England play Australia you want to put up good performances,' he admitted, before twisting the barb by adding, 'We've got exactly what we wanted from [the tour to] Australia.' He went on to suggest to the game's administrators that they should make a greater effort to 'take care' of the global game and 'to find a way to keep it relevant'. He declined to mention the five members of his squad – Mills, Rashid, Hales, Malan and Moeen – who decided to stop on the way home to play in the Abu Dhabi 10 – a contest attracting nobody to the Sheikh Zayed Cricket Stadium other than dutiful media crews and which plumbed virgin depths in terms of meaninglessness.

For it all, nothing could tarnish the achievement of Buttler's side as they met the challenge of winning all of their remaining games after the dampness of Melbourne and the vigour of the Irish. There were no hiccups against either New Zealand or Sri Lanka, but India at Adelaide in the semi-final would, no doubt, test the mettle of any team, probing and exposing any sliver of weakness.

I have written elsewhere about being hobbled by the lowest of expectations when it comes to my sporting affiliations. As I write, my – and I use the possessive pronoun deliberately – football team is enduring its annual grapple with relegation – and possibly even survival. England's footballers, despite the current breed being composed of some apparently very fine young men, never fail to fall frustratingly short of success. I am often pleasantly surprised by the various manifestations of England cricket, but the 29/3 standing joke is born from reality. Memorable victories have historically been carved out of adversity and often seasoned by an energetic rub of the green – McGrath stepping on a cricket ball and four egregious overthrows, for example. So what happened on that memorable Thursday in Adelaide in front of a 40,000 crowd, composed largely of boisterous Indian support, is stamped on the consciousness because of the sheer confidence and self-belief exhibited by a group of sportsmen unprepared to contemplate defeat.

India's healthy total of 168 was battered into the bleachers of the Adelaide Oval at a touch under ten an over and with nobody other than Hales and Buttler having to step out into the middle. Sportspeople are, no doubt, coached by their media team to ensure that semi-final victories elicit no comment other than that of not having achieved anything yet, but three days later, notwithstanding some jittery moments, any such reserve could be abandoned. At an unexpectedly dry MCG, England saw the job through with a five-wicket win against Pakistan. In a reprise of the 2019 50-over final, Channel 4 were granted shared broadcasting rights and so the nation could enjoy this Sunday morning victory, even if a significant number of viewers would have been dismayed by Pakistan doing what they traditionally do so well – not quite being the best Pakistan they can be.

England's two players of Pakistani heritage had made telling contributions throughout the tournament, and this was also the case in the final. Adil Rashid had bowled economically and took two crucial wickets, including the prize of the imperious Babar Azam. Moeen Ali supported a dominant Stokes, joining him at a tentative 84/4, being dismissed with just six needed for victory. He and Rashid embraced, jigged and high-fived with their team-mates, grouped on the podium to receive the trophy and then, depending on the lens through which it was viewed, benefited from a thoughtfully inclusive, well-practised gesture or had their otherness even more firmly signified.

In 2018, following a series win over South Africa in England, captain Alastair Cook had forestalled the mandatory waste of champagne when posing for celebration photographs so that Moeen Ali could be included. It was a moment of cultural awareness that reflected changing behaviour in the international game. When Morgan was asked at the post-2019 World Cup press conference whether he'd had the luck of the Irish, he cheerfully responded by saying that the team 'had Allah with us as well – I spoke to Adil', before going on to attribute the success of the team to its diversity. But when in 2022, Jos Buttler nodded to Moeen and Rashid that the spraying was about to begin, he was either maintaining the sense of awareness installed by Cook and Morgan or reinforcing outdated, privileged and exclusive modes of behaviour. Contrasting reactions did not always originate from predictable sources.

The *About Islam* website commended Buttler's 'classy gesture' and plenty of other news sources from South Asia expressed approval of a respectful understanding of the faith of others. By contrast, *Wisden* online – possibly conscious of its own shaky record on understanding inclusion as we'll see in the final chapter – thought the exclusion of the two Muslim players signalled a time for change. 'When two stalwarts of the team are Muslim,' it opined, 'why is showering the team in alcohol a necessary, immovable part of the celebrations?' In Twitterland, Australian journalist Daany Saeed tartly observed that 'you can't include your mates unless there's booze?' while BBC researcher, Drew Hyndman, was not the only one suggesting that the use of a non-alcoholic substitute would have indicted a move from 'diversity to inclusion'.

It's difficult to look closely at the footage of the presentations and the celebrations without seeing anything other than a group of mates revelling in joint success and each other's company. For a full two minutes they bounce on the podium with Moeen and Rashid front and centre. From there to the sponsors' platform where, after 30 seconds or so, the two players withdraw and join their families while the fizz is sprayed. Moments thereafter, individuals enjoy selfies as they mill around, handing round the trophy and playing with children. There has been no recorded comment from either player about their apparent exclusion, both of whom appear entirely relaxed as they absorb the glorious occasion.

Whether diverse opinion on the champagne moment is the narcissism of the virtue-signalling Twitterati or a genuine contribution to the debate about inclusion is properly contentious. Because you may want to know, I'll furnish the view that I'm happy to take a couple of lagers into my favourite balti house so that I can enjoy them with my seekh kebab without compromising the happily tractable proprietor into stocking unwanted booze. It's an arrangement that suits us both as we go about our business. We're trying not to harm each other – much like Buttler with his valued team-mates. But am I unhappy that such sensitivities are raised, even through the jarring foghorn of quickfire Twitter-bites? Certainly not. Because even as England's players eventually returned home, enduring questions about race and inclusivity were not disappearing from English cricket's agenda any time soon.

Chapter 7

# Back, at last, to Pakistan. Autumn and winter 2022

*To unpathed waters, undreamed shores.*

Camillo: *The Winter's Tale*

ON 13 December, with snow muffling most of the English landscape, cricket's administrators should have been a contented band of brothers and sisters. England's new Test coach may have disowned his side's new label – 'I don't like Bazball, it's a silly term,' McCullum had told the assembled press back in July – but whatever it was called, it was, to borrow from the appropriate terminology, a winning brand. McCullum may have been dismissive of the unwanted tag, but at least the media could relax knowing that they'd get a quote or two out of him. By comparison, England's men's one-day coach, Matthew Mott, was, and remains, almost monastically reserved in his public statements. 'Being in the right place at the right time is a pretty good strategy,' he understated, following the T20 World Cup win in November. England's women emerged from the bumpy summer that had been clouded by their underperformance at the home

Commonwealth Games and, under the new tutelage of Jon Lewis – the man whose playing career was forever blighted by the quip that he was never knowing underbowled – started the new era by making themselves feel a whole lot better by walking through their mismatches with the West Indies with their eyes shut. A World Cup, a series win in Pakistan, a new horizon with some bright young, spiky stars in both the men's and the women's games. Things, as we were once told, could only get better.

Away from play, the ECB was working hard to demonstrate that the upheavals from Azeem Rafiq's revelations were being taken seriously and, on 8 December 2022, published not one, but three reports demonstrating that lessons had been learnt and that strategies were in place to avoid the repetition of mistakes. Acknowledging the 'testimony of those who have experienced discrimination or felt excluded from the game', the board spoke of its determination to recognise that 'Azeem Rafiq ... and the stories of others who have spoken out' had prompted cricket's leaders 'to commit to actions to go further and faster in changing our sport'.

The *Game-wide action plan to discourage discrimination* sat alongside the *Equality, Diversity and Inclusion (EDI) Plan* and the *Comprehensive Action* document. All of this work, the ECB hoped, was contributing to the ambition of making 'cricket a game for everyone'. The three colour brochures – the format now familiar to those of us who had endured the Strauss Report – were by no means the only part of the story. They were forerunners and tone-setters for the Independent Commission for Equity in Cricket (ICEC), established by the ECB 'to examine questions of equity in relation to race, gender and class within cricket' and to report its findings in early 2023 – a commitment that gave new meaning to the term 'elastic' but, as we'll see in the final chapter, turned out to be worth waiting for. Whatever the guardians of the game were doing, the one accusation of which they could not have been found guilty as the year drew to its close, was that it was sitting on its hands.

Way beyond the tiny world of cricket and cricketers, public confidence in those who run major institutions has been diminishing exponentially for some time. A convenient if somewhat arbitrary reference point for when this became most obvious might be the financial crash of 2008. The notion that high finance was controlled by people who had a sensible overview of matters and who knew what they were doing, was revealed as a big, fat lie. Years of privatisation of public services and a governmental penchant for starving local authorities of cash and meaningful decision-making led to many communities, by politicians' own admission, being left behind. The greed, venality and dim-wittedness of some senior politicians was then nakedly exposed during the pandemic with the award of dodgy contracts, vacillation over vital lockdown decisions and, ultimately, the kick in the teeth of the Downing Street parties and the bare-faced lies they spawned. Against this background, asking anybody in the public sphere to produce proof that it is addressing its shortcomings in an open and honest way is a tough demand. For cricket's governing body, by its very nature a byword for stuffy traditionalism, to be challenged in this way is an even greater test. The overload of glossiness, the overkill of three documents, with the promise of a fourth on the way, with the dead hand of corpo-speak extinguishing the reader's will to live, might make the ECB's initial efforts an easy target for ridicule. Which would be unfair.

The reports acknowledged that there remains much to be done. There is clear recognition that establishing community projects that reach into all of cricket's potential constituencies is easy to identify as the key to any success; the energy, commitment and funding required to do so might be another matter. But the message comes loud and clear from the ECB: we know we've mucked this up and we're trying to do something about it – and the glossy brochures are a measure of intent, at least. However good, bad or indifferent their efforts turn out to be will be a matter for time to resolve. And, talking of timing, there might have been a few heads in hands at Lord's as events up at Headingley and down the road in Whitehall unfolded a few days after the reports' publication.

The day after England had finished a compelling tussle in Multan on 13 December with their narrow victory in the second Test, Azeem Rafiq presented further testimony to the parliamentary select committee for Digital, Culture, Media and Sport (DCMS). Before this meeting, and prior to the release of the equality reports, Gary Ballance and Yorkshire County Cricket Club had agreed a mutual termination of his contract, an event that, from the point of view of the county and the ECB, slipped almost unnoticed under the radar of a sporting media still smarting from England's defeat by France in the Qatar World Cup. Ballance, who had previously captained the county, was one of those accused by Rafiq of using racist language – an accusation which he admitted and for which he offered an apology. He had played for England in 23 Tests from 2014, making an extraordinarily promising start, scoring three hundreds and three half-centuries in his first 13 innings at an average of 60.75. Thereafter, with the world's bowlers now apprised by video study of his WG firmness of foot, these high scores became a rarity.

By 2022, his England career was over and his form across the game in red- and white-ball cricket had evaporated. 'On a personal level,' he explained, 'I have gone through a challenging period – and after much discussion, I decided, together with my family, that it would be right to make a change.' He declined to comment on whether the racism accusations had played their part. He was going back to his homeland of Zimbabwe but made no mention of any intended involvement with cricket in the future. He didn't hang around. On 12 January 2023, he made a useful 30 off 29 balls on debut for Zimbabwe against Ireland in Harare, helping his side to a five-wicket victory in a low-scoring T20.

Yet, for it all, neither Ballance's departure nor the ECB's production line of weighty documents managed to reach even the outer reaches of the news headlines. Rafiq's new testimony to the DCMS was the only game in town – and it must have been uneasy listening for Richard Thompson, the ECB chair (yes, we're eventually non-gender-specific), by now four months into his new job. In a teatime interview during the Rawalpindi Test in November, Thompson had been in affable conversation with Jonathan Agnew and had played the deadest of bats to questions about Rafiq's complaints and their implications for the future. His message was as simple as it was evasive: wait for the ICEC report, because I'm not saying anything else. It was probably the voice of a man who knew that despite applying multiple coats of cheap emulsion, the mould would show through soon enough.

The parliamentary select committee session overseeing Rafiq's testimony a few days later opened up new and disturbing ground. This time round, Yorkshire CCC evaded the worst of the opprobrium; that was reserved for the ECB and the *Yorkshire Post*. Rafiq blamed the newspaper for the personal attacks on himself and his loved ones – there had been reports of people circling Rafiq's house with chains, threatening family members and defecating in his parents' garden. He called out what he saw as the paper's over-emphasis on the idea that he had sins of his own to answer for. His view was that not only had the *Post* exaggerated the importance of the exchange of the anti-Semitic messages, it had also been over-enthusiastic in its reporting of alleged incidents of other misconduct, including suggestions, prompted by comments from former England physio Wayne Morton, that Rafiq had been involved in two separate incidents of indecent exposure in 2012. George Dobell, by now confirmed as Rafiq's official biographer, dubbed the paper 'the voice of the racist' and described its cricket correspondent, Chris Waters, as 'out of his depth' for characterising critics of his reporting as 'woke anti-racists'. Dobell was supported in his comments by Kamlesh (Lord) Patel, the chair of the county.

Waters was disinclined to be traduced so publicly and was afforded significant space for a rebuttal in the next day's edition of the *Post*. Calling the DCMS hearing 'a show trial with bells on', he was confidently clear about his own position and of the editorial position of the paper. Referring to Rafiq's testimony about being forced to leave the country because of the racism he had endured, the journalist is vehement in his denial of culpability. 'I repeat – I don't want racism … I don't want people being forced to leave the country. I don't want threats made against them or their families. I don't want people defecating in their gardens. I don't want people circling their houses with what look like chains in their hands. I don't want any of those things.' He's just as adamant that there was, indeed, deep-seated racism at Yorkshire. There was no denying the substance to Rafiq's allegations; there was racist language and unacceptable behaviour from boardroom to dressing room.

Yet what Waters sees lurking behind Rafiq's subsequent actions, and the support from Dobell that this has prompted, are two basic considerations. First, he regards the bowler's intentions as somewhat wider than redressing a personal injustice or even highlighting an important social issue. In December 2021, Yorkshire had presided over a significant clear-out of backroom staff at the behest of the newly installed Patel. The chair had received a letter from a number of employees, some of whom were Britons of Asian heritage, questioning Rafiq's character and what they saw as his 'one-man mission to bring down the club'. The swift sacking of these signatories was characterised by Waters as Patel pulling 'the trigger like a crazed cowboy from the Wild West' before going on to label him 'the worst chairman [sic] in the club's history'. Furthermore, the dismissals had taken place with scant regard for due procedure, which was another element of the episode that stuck in Waters' craw. Although not part of his argument, he could have pointed to how this lack of respect for agreed protocols was a mirror of the conduct of the ECB when it came to industrial relations.

Second, underpinning Waters' argument was his firm belief that he was defending journalistic integrity and probity. 'What I want is to try to do the job of a journalist; I cannot be a cheerleader,' he tells us. His contention was that should he ignore the various shadows that hover over Rafiq's character or decide to gloss over what he saw as hasty, poorly informed and clumsily executed actions by Patel and the Yorkshire board, he would be betraying the cause of credible journalism. The Rafiq affair, he contended, 'is a story of nuance, of context, of many strands'. To skate over this would be unacceptable. 'Although there are sometimes adverse consequences that make us feel uncomfortable, truth must be deemed sacrosanct, and good, impartial, fearless journalism its protector.' He had the firm backing of his editor, James Mitchinson, who was clear in his statement that, 'The *Yorkshire Post* has repeatedly acknowledged the racism suffered by Mr Rafiq and we have been scrupulously objective, impartial and professional in our reporting of the story.'

Which is most definitely not how Rafiq and Dobell saw things. In his testimony to the DCMS in December 2022, Rafiq was unequivocal in his judgement that if he were 'to pick one reason why' the continuing racist abuse occurred, 'I would have to say that it was the *Yorkshire Post*'s reporting.' He was of the view that 'the editorial control and the senior editors … have a lot to answer for.' Dobell proffered his own explanation when agreeing with this: 'I fear that they think they're catering to their market and I'd like to think they've got their market wrong … I think the people of Yorkshire are better than that.' Over in the badlands at Twitter, Dobell received plenty of support for this assertion, although a glimpse at the rogue comments of the minority would make any thinking person's eyes bleed. One thing, however, is certain. In the flurry of whataboutery that masqueraded as debate on social media, particularly those comments emanating from the supporters of the *Post*, the understanding of institutional racism – that it is outcomes and not intentions which should drive our assessment of matters – was as absent there as it was in the spirited obstinacy of Waters and Mitchinson, both in their tweets and on the pages of their paper.

If the ECB members at the hearing were able to allow themselves to breathe relatively easily for a few moments while the *Post* was in the firing line, any such relief was entirely temporary. 'There's a group of people out there who almost feel like cricket's the victim in this,' Rafiq complained. 'I've felt any chance there's been to discredit my experiences, even the ECB have tried to do that.' He was supported in his assertion by Patel, who said of the board that 'every time there's an issue, every time people have needed to stand up and support me, they didn't'. He went on to speak of unanswered calls, letters and emails before accusing the ECB of knee-jerk responses to headlines with no systematic approach to the problems it faced. On the issue of institutional racism, Patel was damning: 'I don't think they do understand it. I don't think the ECB has got it.'

Both Rafiq and Patel were, however, prepared to cut the board a little slack, albeit in the most guarded of ways. 'I've got hope in the new leadership,' the player said, before dampening his statement with the reservation that 'it's very little at present." Similarly, Patel agreed that he was looking forward to the new leadership, but any enthusiasm was constrained by his experience of the last 12 months. Echoing Thompson's comments to Agnew in Rawalpindi, he saw the forthcoming report of the Independent Commission for Equity in Cricket as 'a pivotal moment for the game'. In this, he was at one with the board, who issued a statement saying that the report would 'help to drive the lasting change we need and rebuild trust among communities to show people that cricket can be a game for them'. Rafiq's patience, however, was wearing thin. 'I spoke out to make cricket a better place,' he told the committee. 'Thirteen months on,

I'd have loved to come and tell you how much has changed ... but what it feels like is cricket is in denial.'

How Thompson and his associates must have wished for the time machine to land and whisk them away to the following week. There, in fading light in Karachi, an 18-year-old from Nottingham of Pakistani heritage came out to bat at number three for England. He hit his first ball back over the bowler's head for four and in the next few moments played a succession of hoiks and slashes of unparalleled ugliness before missing with another clumsy swipe and being clean bowled for 10. Of course, Rehan Ahmed had not made his debut for England on the back of his batting prowess, but with the game as good as won, he appeared to have been sent in as the nighthawk – get 30 off 10 of nought off one – as part of new England's madcap mission to reach the target of 167 in the 20-odd overs left in the day. Neither he nor his team-mates were able to earn themselves an extra day off, but as far as Ahmed was concerned, he'd made a pretty impressive stamp on international cricket.

Earlier that day, he had done what every wrist spinner from the Sunday seconds up to Test level does with alarming predictability. Babar Azam, who was batting with unflappable serenity along with Saud Shakeel, seemed to be setting about establishing a challenging target for the fourth innings of the game. Ahmed then cunningly delivered a filthy half-volley which Babar could have chosen to hit anywhere, before deciding that the best thing was to deposit it into the hands of Ollie Pope at shortish midwicket. From there, Ahmed embarked on more respectable ways of picking up wickets before finishing with 5-48, thus breaking the 11-year record held by Australian, Pat Cummins, to become the youngest Test player ever to take five wickets in an innings on debut.

Over at the ECB there must have been mixed emotions. Here was exactly the sort of poster boy they needed. Not only had Ahmed performed so creditably on debut – notwithstanding his rather rustic batting in both innings – but here was a young man who looked entirely at home in Stokes's England. Irrepressible, characterful and, as far as one could discern, very much one of the boys. Two caveats apply, of course. First, all of these positive qualities are easier to display and maintain in a winning side. Second, Ahmed can count himself fortunate to have been selected at a time when both captain and coach had invested much time and energy into the fostering of a team identity. Endless accounts of touring players disappearing to lonely hotel rooms to agonise over performance and prospects pepper their ghosted biographies. On a personal level – and one that is pertinent considering his success in Pakistan – in December 2016 I was in the same hotel restaurant in Mumbai as Ben Duckett and his dad. They were enduring a silent and miserable-looking dinner together. The batter had squeezed out 18 runs in three innings earlier in the tour and had not played for nearly a month. Jollity and camaraderie are in short supply in those circumstances. Ahmed found himself in a very different world.

If the spinner's exploits provided some hope of better messaging about the future for the ECB, Yorkshire too were looking at events in Pakistan to enhance their product. Throughout the summer, Harry Brook had been touted as a future fixture in England's middle order but had found his path blocked by others. Of these, Jonny Bairstow in particular rose to any potential challenge to his place by playing with the fiercely cavalier spirit that Stokes appeared to demand. When he slipped and broke his leg on a tee-box in September, his misfortune allowed Alex Hales his spectacular redemption in the T20 World Cup and created the space for Brook in the Test side. With three centuries, one fifty and 468 runs at an average of 93.60, the 23-year-old exceeded all expectations and prompted some serious agonising for the selectors.

Twenty-four hours after Stokes and Duckett smoothed England's way to unruffled victory in Karachi, Yorkshire decided that the time was right to cash in on their latest favoured son. An email to all their loyal clients – of whom I am one, having once bought a ticket for Headingley – bore the subject 'Brook's brilliance incoming' (no, me neither) and went on to tell us that 'Harry Brook loves a Roses game.' He had 'scored an eye-catching 91 not out' in the Vitality Blast fixture in 2021, following it up with 'another half-century at Old Trafford in 2022'. 'You certainly wouldn't bet against him repeating the feat in 2023,' we are told and so the best way of being there if he does so is to enter the ballot for tickets. Click here. The Roses game in the Blast at Headingley was scheduled for 1 June. As was the opening day of the one-off Test against Ireland. It's unfair to blame the county for squeezing every commercial benefit out of a player for whose development it has been largely responsible, but you can bet its PR team weren't counting on pedants like me checking the cricketing calendar.

As it happened, their prized asset turned out at Lord's, batted for seven balls to see Pope through to a double ton, held on to a regulation catch at point and didn't need to turn his arm over. Up at Headingley, Dawid Malan's 85 paved the way to a Yorkshire victory with three of Lancashire's England stars – Buttler, Salt and Livingstone – mustering 32 runs between them in response. The wunderkind had not been missed.

Brook had been one of the many beacons of hope during a successful autumn and early winter for England's men. The principal focus for the early part of that period may well have been on the World Cup in Australia, but two tours in Pakistan were imbued with their own importance – not least because they represented the settling of important debts within the game. In late September 2021, the ECB had announced that a brief tour of Pakistan – two T20 double-headers involving the men's and women's teams, with the latter staying on for three ODIs – was to be cancelled. New Zealand had called off their own tour a few days earlier, citing security concerns. If this was a worry shared by the ECB, it wasn't one that they specifically mentioned. Their statement invoked 'the mental and physical well-being of our players and support staff [which] remains our highest priority and this is even more critical given the times we are currently living in'. These players had 'already coped with a long period of operating in restricted Covid environments' and so, with reluctance, the decision had been taken not to reciprocate Pakistan's willingness to tour England on two occasions in the preceding 13 months.

In 2020, Pakistan had come to England and played three Test matches and three T20s behind closed doors and under strict quarantine restrictions. A year later, they returned to play three ODIs and three T20s in front of rapt and grateful full houses. Between the start of Covid's global impact in 2020 until the ECB's coy refusal to dance in September 2021, Pakistan's players not only travelled twice to England, but played a full tour in New Zealand and a white-ball series in South Africa as well as Tests and T20s in both Zimbabwe and the West Indies. When Osman Samiuddin wrote on *Cricinfo*'s website that Pakistan was looking at the middle finger of the world's three self-elected cricketing powers – England, Australia and India – when it came to honouring obligations, it was impossible to take issue with his justified indignation. Pouring scorn on commitments to maintain bilateral series, Samiuddin contends that 'what the Big Three mean by more bilateral cricket is bilateral cricket among themselves'. His ire was echoed by Ramiz Raja, chairman (sic) of the Pakistan Cricket Board. 'This is a lesson for us because we go out of our way to accommodate and pamper these sides when they visit … from now on we will only go so far as is in our interest,' he told national media, before going on to identify the 'Western bloc' that exercised its hold over the international game.

And so it was that in November 2021, Tom Harrison was despatched by the ECB to make peace. Press announcements talked with confidence of his meeting both Ramiz along with prime minister and former cricketing great, Imran Khan. Given that no reports followed about such a meeting with the PM, any details about what took place are unclear. The upshot, however, was more certain. It was decided that in the early autumn of 2022, England would play seven – yes, really – T20s in a bilateral series, followed by three Tests in November and December. However, by the time England revealed the latest of their garish outfits to an expectant, packed house in Karachi in September 2022, Harrison was no longer earning his daily bread at the ECB. He probably didn't need to be hotfooting it down to the Job Centre, calculating, no doubt, that his share of the £2.1m paid by the ECB as executive bonuses would see him OK for a while. He had stepped aside in May to mixed reviews about his time in office, but could, at least, have put his feet up as the days shortened to enjoy the spectacle of nearly 190,000 people attending the games – four in Karachi, three in Lahore – with England just about edging a close and engaging series.

Had the tour been born of Harrison's hitherto unlauded diplomatic skills? Given the radio silence about the negotiations, it is impossible to know. What is entirely likely, however, is that a very particular professional diplomat may have had a hand in matters.

During the course of the seven T20s, and for the game at the T20 World Cup Final and the subsequent Test matches, an unlikely star of the small screen emerged. Media appearances of Her/His Majesty's high commissioners must, one imagines, be relatively rare. What's more, any such events might not be the liveliest of affairs. So when Dr Christian Turner, the UK's high commissioner to Pakistan, began popping up for in-match interviews on Sky TV, which turned out to be a prelude to a further period of minor stardom on Pakistani TV news items, it was a happy surprise to be entertained and impressed by the clarity, precision and sheer knowledge on display. And that was even before he startled the home broadcaster by interspersing his comments with fluent Urdu. For TV interviews prior to the World Cup Final, he sported a reversible England/Pakistan shirt while diplomatically – geddit? – joshing with a panel keen to get him to nail his colours to any mast. By the time of these good-natured exchanges, he was nearing the end of his regulation period of office.

To add to his already eye-watering CV, he was to serve from December as director general geopolitical at the UK Foreign Commonwealth and Development Office – a position equivalent to undersecretary of state. Praising his period of tenure in Pakistan, particularly during the floods that swept away the homes and livelihoods of some 15 million people, the UK government website talked of how Turner had 'played a pivotal role in the promotion of sports diplomacy and the return of the England Men's cricket team to Pakistan following a 17-year absence'. Watching his deft conduct during England's exploits, it wasn't hard to guess who might have been doing the heavy diplomatic lifting when it came to getting England back to that part of the world.

Turner must have been putting the final touches to his packing just as Duckett and his captain thwacked and swept away the few remaining runs on the morning of 20 December, wrapping up the 3-0 win in the Test series. Times when a fourth-innings target of 167 might have proved just a touch ticklish had, for the moment, become sooo last decade. A year previously, England had been slouching wearily from a 275-run defeat at Adelaide on their way to an innings defeat at Melbourne, where they were bowled out for 68. By the time they were released from yet another purgatorial Australian episode, they had surrendered the final Test at Hobart with the fidgety haste of pensioners anxious about missing the last bus home. Stokes had scored 9 runs in two innings and hadn't bowled a ball. Who knows if Baz was even a twinkle in the ECB's eye, his last coaching job completed nearly two years earlier as he guided Trinbago Knight Riders to success in the Caribbean Premier League? The new England vintage may have disembarked to a grumpy, underwhelmed sporting nation still raw from Harry Kane's spaceshot penalty, but if they hadn't featured much on the back pages, at least, for the moment, they weren't on the front.

Chapter 8

# Follow the money. How franchises lured the players and grabbed cricket's reins

*There is money, spend it, spend it; spend more; spend all I have*

Ford: *The Merry Wives of Windsor*

THE LIFE of a professional sportsperson is short. A star may fall as rapidly as it rises. In a game where there aren't enough global megastars to constitute a handful, and which has traditionally never reached the foothills of the wages paid to other athletes, even the stuffiest of county members couldn't begrudge a young player shifting his/her left leg from the line of the ball and making hay while the sun shines. And the sun is always shining somewhere. As 2022 drew to its close, nowhere was this universal truth more apparent than in the world of cricket.

Months before the teams of the Indian Premier League were fanfared on to the airwaves in late March 2023 – regaled in kaleidoscopic outfits on which advertisers fought for any inch of vacant space – the franchises that controlled them had already seared their mark on the game and its future. In the first three months of the year, players had multiple 20-over competitions vying for their services. The pay on offer, along with differing conditions, would have dictated their choices, but from South Africa to the Emirates, from New Zealand's low-key Super Smash to their Antipodean neighbours' Big Bash, in Pakistan and over the border in Bangladesh and down to Sri Lanka, there was quick-fire cricket aplenty on offer. Lurking in the treetops or, more likely, hunched over their accounting screens, the game's plutocratic vultures watched and waited – albeit none too patiently. There was money to be made and they weren't going to let any slip away.

With the various leagues overlapping, cricket did what it does best; it made a chaotic set of circumstances even more bewildering. In fairness – and I use the term carefully – the ECB found itself in an invidious situation. Obligated to repay commitments made by those who had accommodated England's wishes, often in demanding circumstances, finding an empty corner of the playground to play a bit of cricket had become a tricky business. At the turn of the year, as the board contemplated its forthcoming commitments in South Africa, Bangladesh and New Zealand, it's not fanciful to think that somewhere in the depths of the ECB's offices at Lord's there might have been a map of the world and, at its centrepiece, a CSI set of connections joining player portraits to particular leagues. As the brains trust pondered this tableau, they'd have had their calculators close at hand as they contemplated their chances of luring their prized assets from the grip of the franchises. Down in the southern hemisphere, one set of cricket executives was probably sitting much more comfortably.

By mid-January, South Africa's SA20 was in full swing and attracting healthy attendances both at grounds and on TV. All six teams were owned by IPL franchises. It's impossible to know how many of those watching as cricket's new puppet masters tightened their grip either knew or cared that the national team had just returned from a Test series in Australia, where they'd been as hapless a set of victims as England the year before – a situation softened for them only by the fact that fewer locals had chosen to come along and revel in their humiliation. Cricket South Africa's decision not to stay for the ODIs and so write off potential World Cup qualifying points, choosing instead to prioritise the launch of their new domestic format, seemed to have been vindicated. At the start of the year, *ESPN*'s Firdose Moonda had headlined her piece by proclaiming that 'SA20 aims to bring light to dark times', referencing the nation's wider anxieties beyond whether the middle order could build decent partnerships. Former Test captain and SA league commissioner Graeme Smith talked of the ambition to 're-energise and revise the cricket fan' and of this being 'a hard job to do in a negative climate'.

For all of his misgivings, Smith and his colleagues at CSA would have been happy enough when, at the second time of asking on the reserve day, Pretoria (Delhi) Capitals took to the field against Sunrisers Eastern Cape (Hyderabad) in front of a packed house for the final at the Wanderers. In a relatively low-scoring game, Sunrisers chased down the 136 needed to win with four wickets and nearly four overs to spare. Their victory was built on the efforts of Adam Rossington, whose 57 off 30 balls established a platform for an otherwise wobbly response. His performance wasn't enough to win him the player of the match award, however: Roelof van der Merwe's

4-31 earned him the £5,000 prize money. Rossington needed to content himself with the divvying up of the £90,000 team prize pot, along with any other perks and pickings along the way. His own contract with Sunrisers was reported as being worth £90,000 and so, by the time he'd packed his kit to return to grey skies and a pile of junk mail, he'd have been satisfied enough with an early winter's work well done. He'd probably not even settled into binge-watching whatever he had lined up before he got the call from Karachi Kings to go and play in the Pakistan Super League.

Rossington, nearly 30 years old, has plied his trade with three counties – Middlesex, Essex and Northants. He's turned out in 103 first-class games at the time of writing and has a batting average of a touch over 34. He's a big lad, which doesn't prevent his wicketkeeping showing nimbleness and agility. He gives it a tremendous biff and so is a valued commodity in T20 cricket, where he has made 121 appearances. 'He can blast an opposition out of the game in no time,' gushes the official website of The Hundred, in whose competition he plays for London Spirit. He had been around the England under-19 set-up but never achieved the step up to the senior squad. If ever there was the personification of the old-fashioned steady county pro, it could have been him. He is emblematic of a game that is no longer undergoing a transformation. The future is now.

Maybe as little as ten years ago, winter may have loomed large for Adam Rossington. Journalist and former Test player, Derek Pringle, recalls the occupations of some who had played at the highest level as they waited for the days to lengthen. Keith Fletcher, who had captained county and country, set up a business selling oil and diesel to local farmers; fast bowler John Lever drove cars from Chelmsford

*England supporters surround Andrew Flintoff at St Kitts. There is a Black person there – the security guard.*

*Allen Stanford smiles and poses with his superstar XI – orange would soon be the central feature of his wardrobe.*

*Joe and Jonny triumphant after their record run chase against India, Edgbaston 2022. Bairstow was in for an interesting few months.*

*World Cup winners 2022. Note the champagne firmly in its place in the corner.*

*Azeem Rafiq speaks to the Commons Select Committee. His revelations lit the blue touchpaper.*

*Anya Shrubsole (centre) celebrates after taking the wicket that wins the 2017 World Cup.*

*An injured Jofra Archer walks his dog. 'The kid lives and breathes cricket,' said Jason Gillespie. Others were more comfortable with lazy stereotypes.*

*England's Amy Jones appeals in vain as Tazmin Brits scores 68 before going on to take three catches, including a worldie, to move into the World Cup Final.*

*Watching cricket at Hove in April. The sort of determination on which empires were built.*

*Will Smeed of the one-match red-ball career. The very model of the modern cricketer.*

*Jubilant West Indies supporters take over The Oval in 1973. Those coppers simply couldn't look happier.*

*May 2023. Luton Caribbean inch toward their winning score of 92 against Milton Keynes Warriors. Just three players of Caribbean heritage are in the current team.*

*Learning from the master. Rehan Ahmed listens carefully to Adil Rashid during England's whistle-stop tour of Bangladesh in March 2023.*

*The ACE squad line up at the Ageas Bowl, with force of nature, Chevy Green, third right.*

*Has he just stepped out of his crease? Rishi Sunak entertains ACE cricketers in the Downing Street garden.*
Image: Simon Walker

'England's Ashes are alive. Test cricket is alive,' gushed Nasser Hussain. Wood and Woakes celebrate at Headingley.

Charlie Dean is mobbed by team-mates having recovered from dropping a catch to run out Tahlia McGrath at the Oval. England won by three runs.

to Scotland for a local dealership; tiny Lancashire batter, Harry Pilling, did a stint as a gravedigger and David 'Bumble' Lloyd was a salesman for a local brewery – whose clients, no doubt, probably just surrendered and bought the stuff to save the ear-bashing. The option of a few weeks in the sun, where the most they'd do was bat for an hour or bowl four overs, could not even have been part of their most fevered imagination. And, yes, of course I'm well aware that I have over-simplified the nature of the requirements for those playing in the franchises, but you could forgive any eye-rolling from ex-players muttering that the new breed didn't know they were born.

If there is a residual sniff of the county circuit around Adam Rossington, no such fragrance lingers over the presence of that very model of the modern cricketer, William Conrad Francis Smeed. In November 2022, 21-year-old Smeed was probably responsible for promoting some serious thrombosis risk among cricket's geriatrati when he announced his retirement from the red-ball game without ever having played it – always allowing for a two-ball duck in his one game for England Lions. 'I think there will be grumbling among the traditionalists,' he told the *Telegraph*, before going on to express the ambition to 'become the best white-ball player I can, and the sacrifice is playing red-ball cricket'. In an extensive interview with *The Cricketer*, he talked of the value of being around players like Moeen Ali and Liam Livingstone when playing for Birmingham Phoenix, with the guiding hand of Kane Williamson in the dugout. The sole, collective intention of this brains trust was to 'give it a go'. In an observation sure to infuriate some of the protectors of the game, his comment that his approach in The Hundred 'wasn't massively technical – I wasn't after anything technical' but simply copying experienced team-mates who 'approach batting [in a way that] works for them,' would have had many a wizened coach harrumphing in disapproval.

To underline the point, Smeed – privately educated – seems affable, intelligent and properly ambitious and appears to have his head screwed on. He is not the cricketer of the future, but the cricketer of the present. He finishes his *Cricketer* interview by reiterating his aspirations. Opening the batting for England? Being part of an Ashes-winning team? Afraid not. His objectives are two-fold: to make sure that he bats through the 20 overs whenever possible and to do so at T20 'Finals Day, if I get the opportunity'.

During the break in the bolt-on ODIs between South Africa and England that rudely interrupt SA20 in late January 2023, Atherton and Hussain sit in the home-based studio and reflect with Ian Ward on the game and its direction of travel. Both are unequivocal in their judgement that the landscape of the game has changed and that refusal on the part of administrators to recognise this would be an act of self-harm. Neither quite go as far as saying that the traditional spectator had just better get used it, but that is almost implicit in their assessments. 'It's not about three old fogeys sitting on a red sofa and saying "in our day …"' observes Hussain, before going on to state the obvious: TV companies, franchises and advertisers are now the dominant influences on how, where and when the game is played. He is not grizzling: he's stating plain fact. And there are a couple of other truisms that are to be dismantled.

Of these, perhaps the most alarming for traditionalists is the fact that representing your country is no longer the pinnacle of a player's aspiration. In almost all major sports, decisions not to play for the national team, to prioritise club commitment or to exercise plain old personal preference, have conventionally been met with the same response. To torture a couple of metaphors, the historical attitude of selectors and committees has been that boats have been burned and doors will never again be darkened. In the new world of multi-format, globally franchised cricket, that's just not going to wash. Hussain is clear that the precedence of national selection is no longer tenable when the fees paid by franchises for top players outstrip even the most generous of offers from international teams. Atherton reinforces this assessment: 'When the free market hits the established, representative game, the free market will always win.' At almost the same time as they were speaking, another illustrative episode was playing out and at its centre, once again, was Alex Hales.

In January 2023, Hales announced that he had been given permission to miss out on England's forthcoming white-ball tour of Bangladesh in favour of playing in the Pakistan Super League for Islamabad United. The *Telegraph* quoted sources that the ECB were 'highly understanding of the situation' and had made it clear that he could definitely be part of the planning for the 50-over World Cup later in the year. Coach Matthew Mott was equally open to such a possibility. 'He's a proper cricketer,' he said of the opener, 'and there's absolutely no reason why he couldn't get in the 50-over team.' Hales's contract with Islamabad was reported to be worth about £140,000; his fee for playing for England in Bangladesh was set at £25,000. At 34 years of age and with no obstruction from the ECB, his decision would not have been difficult. The best of both worlds was on offer; to refuse would have been unfathomable.

All of which, in this new era of moneyed commitment juggling, would have been fine, had it not been for a very modern dimension added to the mix. In mid-February, having whacked 82 off 54 balls in his first innings in the PSL, Hales announced that he'd been defeated by bubble-life and hotel living and was calling it a day. In his resignation statement, he talked of being subject to restrictions during the Big Bash which had been unexpected and of how the 'PSL bubble has been understandably very strict and it has just all caught up with me.' He had already made his decision not to renew his contract with IPL franchise, Kolkata Knight Riders.

While it may make good sport for the millions of us whose wage slavery tricks us into thinking that making a living by playing a game in permanent sunshine has to be the very life of Reilly, Hales's predicament, like that of many of his fellow professionals, is now well documented and universally recognised. A few days later, he was followed by Ben Duckett, tweeting that he needed to forgo his contract with Quetta Gladiators to get home to friends and family. As they dusted down their suitcases, replacements were whistled up from the cab rank. Two Wills, Jacks at Islamabad and Smeed at Quetta, stepped into their shoes. Hales's recovery was speedy: he re-joined Islamabad at the start of March.

Meanwhile, the utter confusion of the selection of England's squad for Bangladesh was summed up in a few lines from *Wisden* online in early February. 'It's nearly impossible to tell,' explained Katya Witney, 'who has been dropped from the ODI squad.' Some players had full commitments to the PSL while others were hedging their bets, shuffling their feet skittishly in different camps. Joe Root was not included, struggling, by his own admission, to establish a role in the franchises while temporarily uncertain about where his style fitted with Bazball. Wonderboy Brook was going to Pakistan and only Olly Stone would have been able to unravel the mystery of whether he was fit or not.

But if this confusing jumble was all getting too much, down in Mount Maunganui in mid-February, Jimmy and Broady got the plump old Barmies clapping and singing along as they continued to rattle the wicket-taking counter. All was for the best in the best of all possible worlds. The symphonic refrain that Test is Best rang in our ears, however much the cheap, jangling carousel of commercialised cricket was trying to suggest otherwise. That games of cricket were even taking place in a country recovering from the ravages of catastrophic flooding in the wake of Cyclone Gabrielle was something of an eyebrow-raiser. New Zealand seamer, Blair Tickner, brought a sense of perspective by observing that, 'Cricket doesn't feel hard when you see livestock on the side of the road dead, people crying, their whole lives turned upside down … cricket is my life but it's nothing compared to what people are going through at the moment.'

For some in England's touring party, there may have been a sense of deja vu, having left Pakistan where, despite being cotton-woolled in their secure bubble, they'd have been fully aware that climate disaster had provided a grim backdrop to their exertions. There's a possibility that those lounging on the grass banks at the Bay Oval might have done a bit of carbon offsetting for their own journey. All the same, cricket's relationship with global warming, along with that of all major sporting bodies, remains largely unexamined.

At the end of 2022, Robert Wilby from Loughborough University headed up a research report on the impact of sport emissions on climate for the New York Academy of

Sciences. It started with a recognition that the relationship between top-level sport and climate change was one that still required significant attention, but there was no escaping the need for such investigation. 'As a global industry,' the report states, 'sport makes potentially significant contributions to climate change through carbon emissions and influence over sustainability practices.' It considers the possibility of the effectiveness of legislation aimed at 'energy intensive tournaments and global sports-tourism providers'. The closing sentence suggests that 'perhaps the time has come for a new Olympic motto. Rather than "*Citius, Altius, Fortius*" ("Faster, Higher, Stronger"), we now need "*Tardius, Proprius, Leviora*" ("Slower, Closer, Lighter") footprints.'

Their principal findings were aimed at the so-called Mega Sports Events – the Olympics and the World Cup – particularly in terms of the expansion of infrastructure required to host such gatherings and, just as pertinently, to shift hundreds of thousands of spectators around the globe. While a few planeloads of Brits seeking some winter sun in the southern hemisphere might not provide the last-straw dose of pollution that tilts the world to final catastrophe, cricket's authorities, along with those of all major sports, may yet need to question itself about the necessity of shifting large entourages to four distant countries in the space of six months. Given the manic nature of its global calendar, what's good for player welfare could yet be good for that of the planet as well.

In the temperate lull after the storm, those who paid the suitably modest sums to watch the two Tests at the Bay Oval in Mount Maunganui and at Wellington's Basin Reserve would have been happy punters. In the first of these, England continued to bash away at five an over,

Broad and Anderson took 12 wickets between them, Brook gave another masterclass in early-21st-century batting and England came away with a thumping 267-run victory. The juggernaut then rolled on to a Wellington pitch which jolted TV viewers into wondering whether they'd gone back to the old days of needing to adjust the colour contrast, so little differentiation was there between the greenness of the wicket and the surrounding playing area. Sure enough, an hour after having been inserted, there we were – England 29/3 and looking at scraping together 150 to maybe make a game of it. Nothing to see here. Time for bed.

Only to wake and find that no further wickets had fallen, that Brook and Root had both scored centuries and that, following the early setbacks, we were back to five an over and looking at something in excess of 450 in the first innings. With typical bravado, Stokes declared once Root reached 150 and within moments, New Zealand were 7/2 and then 21/3. They crept to 138/7 by the close but this was a game that was now so firmly in England's grasp that the outcome was inevitable.

Except, of course, it wasn't. In the morning, some clean farmyard hitting from Southee eroded the healthiness of the lead. All the same, when Stokes defied modern convention by enforcing the follow-on with England 226 runs ahead, his decision was met with unqualified approval. This was proof positive that new England were not playing by any stale old rules and with residual green tinge aplenty and the bowlers still happily fresh, this would all be wrapped up pretty soon. It was at that point that Test cricket perked up and in its cheery, transgressive way made fools of us all.

With the unfussy grit that made them world Test champions, New Zealand ground out 483 at an old-fashioned three runs an over, with the epitome of modest, uncomplicated orthodoxy, Kane Williamson, leading the way. The bodies of Anderson and Broad obeyed science not hype as their pace dropped and the venom evaporated. Despite a collapse during which New Zealand lost their last five wickets for 28, England were left with over a day to score the 258 needed to win.

It's worth taking a moment to reflect on this. During the summer of 2022, England chased scores of 279, 299 and 296 to beat New Zealand, culminating in them gambolling away to score 378 in the one-off Test against India. At the end of that extraordinary achievement, the eighth-highest chase in Test history, Stokes joked that he'd have liked to have been set more, just to see if they could get them. All of which meant that somewhere in the mindset of England's followers, the notion had been lodged that hunting down a modest 258 had all become ploddingly routine. This could possibly tell us something about the fragility of collective memory – something on which elements of our political class seem to rely – but those of us who regularly follow the national team had borne too many scars to take anything so lightly. It turned out that our scepticism was well founded, although the journey to the confirmation of our suspicions proved once again that sport truly is the greatest of unscripted dramas.

On the morning of the fifth day, after Crawley's crooked bat, Duckett's wild slash and nighthawk Ollie Robinson's ugly hoik had reduced England to 59/3, Ollie Pope and Root looked calm enough as they set about playing some lively, but sensible cricket. At one point, they set of for a dodgy single, thought better of it and got back grinningly in time. 'Every collapse needs a run-out,' joshed New Zealand commentator, Debbie Hockley, before referencing the dozy dismissal of Michael Bracewell the previous evening. A few moments later, once Pope had departed, Root so thoroughly barbecued his golden boy successor that it was a surprise not to see Brook depart with a splodge of brown sauce down his shirt front. Out without scoring and without facing a ball. The cricketing deities had had their sport with him as they did in a different way with Neil Wagner. After a gruesome display of pie-chucking in the first innings and having failed to score a run at two attempts, it was the combative fast bowler who took the key wickets of Root and Stokes, then grabbed an excellent catch to dismiss Ben Foakes and sealed the most thrilling of victories when Anderson must have thought he'd clipped the winning runs but was strangled down the leg side.

In the aftermath of New Zealand's one-run victory – only the second time a Test had been won by such a margin – reaction from all corners spoke of a game that was coming to terms with how to protect its prized, traditional format. Despite his obvious and justifiable joy at winning, New Zealand's captain, Tim Southee, was firm in his acknowledgement of the part his opponents had chosen to play. 'It's great for Test cricket the way England have been playing,' he told the post-match media conference. 'All the guys cherish Test cricket and hopefully having matches like this will be good for Test cricket going forward.' One of Stokes's predecessors, Alastair Cook, introduced a note of characteristic reserve. Asked about the decision to enforce the follow-on, he said of the captain that, 'He does think about things in a different way, but when it gets to the crunch of an Ashes series, I think it will be slightly different … but not much.' Stokes's declaration on the first day of the Ashes Test showed that it wasn't much at all.

All of this happened after Atherton and Hussain's couch analysis of some of the accepted truisms of the game that are now struggling for breath. Both had accepted that by-passing the offer of playing for your country no longer meant cricketing death along with the notion that, whisper who dare, there were now people associated with the game who might just be challenging its most revered doctrine. There were voices around suggesting that Test cricket might not represent the game's unarguable zenith. Even before the drama at Wellington, they'd have been fully aware that to even suggest such a thing was, quite simply, beyond the pale, an affront to the game's greats and their opinion.

When he hung up his bat, Sachin Tendulkar had reminded the press pack that 'Test cricket ... is where the real cricket is according to me ... Test cricket is cricket of the highest level.' In his collection of players' tales about 'the enduring spirit of the baggy green', Jesse Hogan quotes Stuart Law on getting his only shot at wearing it. While expressing regret at not having further opportunities, Law is adamant in his appreciation of its value. 'Everyone should know – and needs to know – that everyone who puts that baggy green on absolutely loves the fact that they're representing your country and that you'd try your nuts off and do everything for it. You're part of the family.' The crowds who pack the stands in England to watch any Tests, those Australians who do so for the Ashes (when they're winning) and those who use their pensions as they'd always intended to contribute to global warming – none of them/ us need any convincing. For a few heady hours at the Basin Reserve, those present and the insomniacs watching on TV were witnessing iron proof that we were watching a spectacle supplied by the gods. But despite Baz and Ben doing their level best to keep it 21st-century, how healthy is this particular parrot?

Follow the money. In January 2023, Tristan Lavalette, writing in *Forbes* magazine, observed that 'it's admirable that Australia still put Test cricket on a pedestal'. Had he witnessed the lame manner of their collapse from 95/3 to 114 all out in Delhi a few weeks later, he may have reached a different conclusion. It certainly wasn't to the liking of the platoon of former Aussie players lining up to berate the gutlessness of their pampered, impatient successors. But Lavalette's judgement that 'other nations [are] … reading the writing on the wall' was firmly on the money. At around the same time, Fergus Ryan of the *Financial Times* pointed out that 'to the media companies, the long format of the game is not as valuable as it was or as popular as one-day internationals and the even shorter T20'. With privateers circling the Big Bash and The Hundred, the measly pickings from a few days' jollity in the emerald green of the late New Zealand summer wouldn't be on the radar of cricket's money men. We'll look later on at how Bazball is an overt recognition of this reality, but even if the red-ballers maintain their run-a-ball pace, the sleep of franchise owners will remain smoothly untroubled.

In the wake of the derring-do at Wellington, it might have come as a surprise to some cricket aficionados to wake up the next day and remember that England were playing again. To the credit of the ECB, the tour of Bangladesh took place in order to fulfil an obligation that had been reneged upon in the autumn of 2022. So it was that three ODIs and three T20s were played out in just under a fortnight in front of appreciative, and increasingly triumphant, fans in Mirpur and Chittagong.

The England machine seemed to be rolling effortlessly along, wrapping up the ODI series after two games in Mirpur, with the bonus of Jason Roy locating the middle of his bat and Jofra Archer and Mark Wood consistently hurtling up speeds of more than 90mph. Rehan Ahmed became the youngest player to make his debut for England in this format and the home side's record of not having lost a bilateral series in this format on their own turf for seven years came to an end. With frustrating inevitability, James Vince looked lithe and elegant in his failures in an England shirt, before becoming top scorer in the dead rubber at Chittagong, which England lost chasing 247, setting the tone for the sloppiness that characterised their remaining games of a long winter.

Having never beaten England in the T20 format, Bangladesh reeled off three victories on the bounce on tricky, sticky tracks that denied the free swingers their customary opportunity to trust the bounce and hit merrily through the line into the bleachers. In April 1967, less than a year after England won the football World Cup, Scotland went to Wembley and defeated the world champions 3-2 and, with mischievous justification, declared themselves successors to that title. There was no such triumphalism from the courteous and grateful hosts, notwithstanding the vigour and inventiveness of some players' celebrations. England's captain Jos Buttler, almost certainly by now longing for either frost or drizzle, was not outwardly downhearted. A few clichés about seeing what certain guys did under pressure and learning about … insert as necessary … and home for a few weeks other than those who would find themselves in the IPL razzmatazz before they knew it.

The coverage of the games in Bangladesh was hard to find as bloated football gobbled up the sports pages and TV bulletins. But cricket still managed to find its way into the news. Early in March, while Dawid Malan was grinding out his dogged match-winning century in Mirpur, the Cricket Disciplinary Committee met in London to consider charges against six Yorkshire former players and staff accused of racist behaviour towards Azeem Rafiq and other players of South Asian heritage. Having expressed a lack of confidence in the proceedings, almost all of those accused chose not to attend. Besides Michael Vaughan – who opted to be there in person – the most high-profile of these players were former internationals, Tim Bresnan and Matthew Hoggard. Their decision to absent themselves might well have been based on their reluctance to hear reference to having called Rafiq's sister a 'fit Paki' or of calling the bowler 'Rafa the Kaffir' along with japes about a 'token black man' as well as the habitual use of 'you lot' when speaking about some of their colleagues.

Banter, of course. Hoggard, unlike Bresnan who had previously told the ECB that he had never used such language, admitted to some such usage, but denied that he had done so in a way that had discriminatory intent. For Jane Mulcahy, counsel for the ECB, Hoggard's suggestion that this was all simply part of robust dressing-room culture in less enlightened times was, in itself, further proof of a wider culpability. 'This is consistent with Yorkshire's admission that it failed adequately to address systemic use of racist or discriminatory language over a prolonged period,' she told the hearing.

During his rest day in Bangladesh, Adil Rashid supplied testimony to a hearing which elicited little coverage until Michael Vaughan arrived at the International Arbitration Centre in Fleet Street the next day. The accusation that the former England captain had made a racist comment towards four Yorkshire players prior to a game in 2009 had become the principal point at issue. Rashid, who had offered overt support for Rafiq in his claims about the club's institutional racism, did not deliver any kind of *coup de grace* in his testimony. Vaughan's comments – the precise nature of which were subject to some dispute – were, Rashid suggested, a 'bad joke … a poor attempt at humour'. He had not been offended and did 'not believe that [Vaughan] is a racist or that this was said with any bad intention'.

When questioned by Mulcahy, Vaughan opted for the front-foot approach. He 'couldn't have been more proud' to be leading such a diverse team; it was inconceivable that he would say anything to team-mates to 'put them in a bad state of mind' before trying to win a game of cricket. On the issue of an historic tweet from 2010 when the cricketer had complained about being unable to understand a call-centre operative, he admitted behaving poorly, 'but when I do something wrong, I stick my hand up and say I'm wrong'. He expressed his frustration at having become embroiled in what he called 'word-versus-word' process from 14 years ago, along with his regret that his own involvement – which he forbore to mention had pretty well ended his career with the BBC – was a 'bad look' for the game.

In that, irrespective of any other truths or uncertainties, he was indisputably correct. With Australia having redeemed themselves in spectacular style in Indore and talk of the Ashes just about infiltrating the discourse as the last England cricketer returned from international duty, the hornets' nest identified and agitated by Azeem Rafiq wasn't showing any signs of being becalmed.

Chapter 9

# Don't blush, baby. Women's cricket – no longer a sideshow, but still fishing in a puddle

*And all the men and women merely players*

Jacques: *As You Like It*

ON 4 January 2016, Chris Gayle, probably the most treasured bat-for-sale in the world at the time, gave a masterclass in misreading the room. In an in-play interview during Channel Ten's coverage of the Big Bash, he cringingly propositioned Australian broadcaster, Mel McLaughlin. It's possible that lines about beautiful eyes and invitations to have a drink later have served the international superstar well enough over the years. It's just about conceivable that the sort of instant recoil shown by McLaughlin may have been softened by imprecations not to blush. But if it had ever worked before, it only made his boorishness even more evident on this occasion. With the true arrogance of a man who habitually refers to himself in the third person, Gayle departed the scene unruffled and, no doubt, thinking himself the finest of fellows.

His insouciance was not shared by those either playing or commentating on the game. There was an instant rebuttal from the TV commentary team and within the hour, Anthony Everard, the head of the Big Bash League, tweeted that Gayle's comments were 'disrespectful and simply inappropriate'. The chief executive of Gayle's team, Melbourne Renegades, assured followers that he'd be speaking to the player and that there was 'just no place for that sort of behaviour'. Andrew Flintoff chipped in by expressing his general admiration for Gayle but that, on this occasion, he 'made himself look a bit of a chop'. Female colleagues of McLaughlin lined up to condemn Gayle as not funny, smooth, clever or original, with all of them praising the journalist's calm professionalism. If there was any lingering doubt about the unacceptability of the player's conduct, it came in the form of the support offered by serial needy dimwit, Piers Morgan, who expressed outrage at the disapproval heaped on a player who was just 'being a bit cheeky to a female TV reporter'.

We could choose to be charitable here. Setting aside the propensity of the likes of Gayle and Morgan to pine for lost worlds dominated by the certainty of unchallenged male dominance, it may be that they'd just not quite caught up with the idea that women were now playing some high-standard cricket in established leagues. Among these was the Women's Big Bash League (WBBL), in its inaugural season at the time of Gayle's poorly judged advances. A few months later, the Women's Kia Super League was launched in the UK. England stars Charlotte Edwards and Heather Knight, who had vied with, but lost out to, the titan that is Meg Lanning as the highest rated player in the WBBL, swapped Perth Scorchers for Southern Vipers and Hobart Hurricanes for Western Storm respectively. The franchise merry-go-round was most definitely no longer a male preserve.

In 2015, Claire Connor, then the head of women's cricket at the ECB, welcomed reports indicating increased participation among girls and women and talked of plans to 'normalise' such involvement. Unsurprisingly, she had to acknowledge the same accessibility issue that dogged the men's game – most female players had found their way to the game from either private education or family connections to established clubs – but was undaunted by the challenge. 'There are conservative attitudes in all sports,' she explained to the *Guardian*, 'but you can't just appeal to half the population ... you have to promote the game to everyone.' A couple of years later in 2017, on a frenzied July afternoon at Lord's, she'd have parked her concerns for a while at least.

There, at the 50-over World Cup Final, in front of an increasingly boisterous crowd, of which the majority were girls and women, England posted a relatively modest 229 – a total that seemed to be confirmed as inadequate as India rollicked along to 191/3, requiring a further 39 from seven overs with seven wickets in hand. Thirty-four balls, 28 runs and six wickets later, seamer Anya Shrubsole bundled and grunted her way to the end of her allotted spell and clean bowled Rajeshwari Gayakwad for a duck to win the game. She had finished with 6-46, battling through a final spell that was informed as much by a sheer, cussed will to win as it was by her great skill and ability. In the months that followed, she was nominated for BBC Sports Personality of the Year and then became the first woman to grace the cover of *Wisden* the following spring. On that day at Lord's, along with her ecstatic team-mates, Shrubsole was at the centre of the celebrations, providing the very heroines that so many in the crowd would be idolising and imitating.

There's no way of knowing how many spectators that day had any grasp of the background of the victors in front of them. For many, the brand of modern, multi-form cricketer was all they would have known. In much the same way that top-flight football employs Stalinist revisionism that insists there was once football and then there was the Premier League, cricket – and women's cricket in particular – could justifiably argue that a new era of professionalism probably emerged with the new century. It's certainly true to say that, historically, TV executives around the world had not been thinking about how to build their portfolio around acquiring this niche product.

Women have played competitive cricket in England dating back to the late 19th century, but it was not until 1934 that Test cricket between women's teams from England and Australia began. That contest was not deemed worthy of being designated as the 'Women's Ashes' until England's home series in 1998. A clumsy attempt at replicating some burnt remains resulted in bat-scorching with the residue placed in a hollow ball as the prize, but by 2013 this homespun remnant was replaced by a bona fide trophy. Part of the reason for such bounteous recognition was the introduction of the multi-format competition – a combination of Tests, T20s and ODIs with points allocated on a sliding scale. After initial success in this set-up both home and away in 2014 and 2015, England's women, despite their heroic efforts in 2023, have been unable to wrest the trophy from an increasingly dominant Australia. Their opportunities for doing so are diminishing with the passage of time along with the prevailing appetite for the shorter game among spectators and broadcasters.

In August 2022, the International Cricket Council (ICC) announced its Future Tours Programme (FTP) for the women's game. Covering the period until 2025, the launch of the programme was heralded on the council's website with the promise of 'more Test match cricket between countries'. Which was only sort of true. *The Cricketer* headlined its report on the FTP with the announcement of 'further Test matches written into inaugural women's Future Tours Programme' and hailed 'the show of commitment to the longest format from Cricket Australia'. ICC general manager, Wasim Khan, was quoted as describing the programme as 'a huge moment for the women's game'. That may well have been the case, but probably more relevant was Khan's observation that 'this FTP not only lends certainty to future cricket tours, but also sets the base for a structure that is sure to grow in the coming years'.

The detail of that more solid structure is revealing. Any apparent commitment to Tests wasn't easy to discern. 'In total, there will be over 300 international women's games,' the website proudly announced. Well, that part was indisputable. There were to be 301 games, in fact, between ten nations scheduled until April 2025. Of these, 159 were T20s and 135 were ODIs, leaving seven Test matches. Six of the ten nations wouldn't play in such games. England would do so on five occasions, Australia on four, South Africa three and India would do so twice. That makes 2% of fixtures scheduled over the next 30 months being dedicated to women's Test cricket – representing such stark writing on the wall that anyone failing to read and understand these figures really does need to seek the services of the high street opticians of their choice.

The likelihood of anyone other than the most deprived of cricket nerds (guilty) waiting nervously for the release of the FTP is beyond slim. Had any unhinged aficionado been doing so, however, they'd already have been forewarned about its contents as they related to women's Test cricket. A couple of weeks earlier, Greg Barclay, the independent chair of the ICC, had fired the clearest of warnings. 'If you look at the way cricket is going, there is no doubt that white ball is the way of the future – that is the game that is being sought by the fans, where the broadcaster are putting their resources and what is driving the money.' He expressed doubts about the existence of any domestic structures that could possibly provide the foundation for women's Tests before voicing his opinion that he didn't 'really see [Test cricket] as part of the landscape moving forward to any real extent'.

It is impossible to argue with Barclay's reasoning or his conclusions. Test match cricket, played by either men or women, may well remain the undisputed apogee for many of us who came to it in a variety of ways and backgrounds. There remains plenty of evidence that, on a good day with a following wind, younger people will also find their way to this obvious decision. But in a time of multi-platformed sport, available on a range of devices and presented to audiences that could stray in an instant with an impromptu click or swipe, cricket has to fight its corner for its share of spectators and, just as importantly for those of us who love it, its future participants. For the majority of those belting out their appreciation as Shrubsole's inswinger knocked back Gayakwad's off stump – and who will make up significant swathes of the audience for the women's Hundred – white-ball cricket has formed and cemented their love for the game.

For lovers of the traditional game, the challenge is to see it through a different lens. By way of an illustration, some 20 years ago, schools, colleges and universities needed to learn how to best harness the enormous possibilities that came with new digital technologies. Teachers, like parents, had to sharpen up to make use of these wonderful resources and to keep at least one step ahead of increasingly savvy learners. Laden though it may sound to contemporary ears, the labels of 'digital immigrants' and 'digital natives' served to capture this phenomenon. Grandparents who have witnessed children attempting to swipe a conventional TV screen will be acutely aware of the fitness of these descriptors. People who now come fresh to the modern game, untrammelled by any knowledge or acquaintance of what has gone before, know what cricket is and what it looks like. Shorter – and shortest – forms are not deficit models of the real thing: they *are* the real thing.

We've seen in earlier chapters that establishing the conditions for getting young people interested in cricket, irrespective of gender, is riven with problems largely related to class and race. The women's game, particularly at the top level, is equally beset by such problems.

In February 2023, England's women defied usual expectations in their T20 World Cup performances. Instead of stumbling somewhere along the way in the group stages so that they had to play knockout cricket earlier than needed, and then overcoming someone in a tough game in the semis before going on to lose to Australia in the final, they introduced a new variation. Having effortlessly topped their group, defeating India on the way, they duly avoided Australia in the semis and were drawn against the stuttering hosts, South Africa, who had suffered a surprise defeat at the hands of Sri Lanka in the opening game. Having defeated them in every one of their five previous outings in T20s since July 2022, England were clear favourites.

South Africa's 164 on a benign Newlands wicket looked a decent proposition. But even when Sophia Dunkley plopped a sitter into the hands of Tazmin Brits, she'd already set the tone for a 10-an-over response that would soon wipe it away. Up in the hospitality boxes, Claire Connor was smilingly relaxed as England embarked on their path to the final. And then, no doubt as part of their quest for complete parity with their male counterparts, England's women paid homage to that most characteristic of the nation's traditions, the unnecessary collapse. Which is disrespectful to the verve and ability demonstrated by South Africa's bowlers and fielders as they revelled in the increasing exuberance of their supporters.

Quick bowler Shabnim Ismail has clearly learnt from the fast bowlers' playbook that demands unashamed, demonstrative hatred of batters. Fired into eye-bulging fervour by her dismissal of Dunkley, it was the head and helmet of incomer Alice Capsey that were now firmly in her crosshairs. The England batter was not to be cowed, slapping her second delivery firmly to midwicket only to stand aghast as Brits grabbed a breathtaking catch at full length, inches from the ground. Twenty minutes later, Danni Wyatt, breezing along at just over a run a ball, clipped Ayabonga Khaka round the corner where Brits tumbled into action to snap up another tricky chance. And then just as Heather Knight and Nat Sciver-Brunt seemed to have found the rhythm to win the game, the latter didn't quite get enough on her lofted drive down the ground. Any hope she – and England – may have had of a reprieve evaporated immediately when it was clear that it was Brits standing coolly underneath it, her feet a good few inches inside the boundary and her eyes watching the ball all the way into her hands.

Brits had already made a significant mark on the game with 68 from 55 balls: it wouldn't have taken the adjudicators long to decide that she was player of the match. Of her magnificent piece of athleticism to dismiss Capsey, her memories were hazy. 'My legs were so tired after the batting,' she revealed, 'I just reacted and it stuck.' A former javelin thrower, she had been forced away from the event by a car crash prior to the 2012 Olympics, making her cricket debut for South Africa in 2018 at the age of 27. Being so steeped in competitive sport, she'd have known that the cricketing gods would have the last laugh.

In her team's defeat to Australia in the final, she held on to a regulation skier to dismiss Ellyse Perry but could only scratch her way to 10 from 17 before clunking her mishit drive to mid-on. For a woman who had overcome a fractured pelvis and hip as well as puncturing her bladder in the accident that ended her Olympic dream, she'd more than fulfilled her obligation as a role model. When it later emerged that she'd insisted on returning to the field of play following Capsey's dismissal, her role as superwoman was even more fully assured. 'When I dived, I thought it was a vein that popped, it stood out, but they pushed it down … we weren't sure if it was a bone or not … but I said to [our physio] please let me go back on the field.'

England's Heather Knight reached for the defeated captain's playlist with admissions of being 'gutted' while commending the very good plan of their opponents. They would, of course, 'come back stronger', secure in the knowledge that 'this game doesn't define us as a group.' Knight probably made the final comment meaning to do nothing more than reference the close-knit relationship of the players – although that had looked a touch precarious while Katherine Sciver-Brunt was berating her colleagues for fielding errors late in South Africa's innings. The England captain certainly wasn't talking about the social and ethnic composition of the squad, but that is a dimension definitely worth exploring.

Of the 11 players who started the semi-final in Cape Town, four were educated at non-selective state secondary schools. All made connections to established local clubs from either school or family. Only one identifies as a person of colour. In this, the make-up of England's team is a reflection of the wider women's set-up. At the start of the World Cup, some 23 women were on contracts of varying value. Of these, 15 were either independently or selectively educated and all had found their way to top-level cricket through connections with clubs. All of this speaks of a background of disposable income, active parental support – most often in the form of perpetual taxi services – and a degree of social capital. If these preconditions didn't represent a sufficiently demanding set of criteria, the wider context of enabling girls and women to access sport is just as challenging.

In the summer of 2022, the charity Childwise commissioned a report that confirmed suspicions that the surge of enthusiasm for girls' participation in team sport following the success of football's Lionesses could fizzle out without careful nurturing. In a survey of 2,700 schoolchildren aged 5–16, it emerged that girls in secondary schools played half the amount of football, rugby and cricket as boys. The figures for primary schoolchildren were not quite so stark, with more than half the girls surveyed playing football compared to 80% of boys. But when it came to actual numbers, particularly in terms of cricket, the figures are grim. Although around 20% of both boys and girls in primary schools received some cricket coaching, these figures drop to 21% of boys and just 12% of girls at secondary level. In terms of a reservoir from which to draw, that's a puddle, not a pool.

When it comes to the ethnic composition of England's team, along with the broader issue of widening participation, the ECB acknowledges the problem. In its *South Asian Action Plan* it talks of there being no 'quick fix' and of involving 'a mix of short-term actions alongside medium- and long-term ambitions'. There is recognition that 'key partners' will be crucial although it fails to identify who these may be, which, given the influential role played by Ebony Rainford-Brent's ACE (African Caribbean Engagement) programme – as we'll soon see – seems to be something of a careless omission. There are, however, all the right noises coming from the great and the good when it comes to the need to address the issue.

In its comprehensive report of 2019, *Transforming Women's and Girls' Cricket*, the ECB's glossy pamphlet is littered with uplifting comment from a range of stakeholders. Heather Knight talks of enabling girls and women 'to see a clear pathway ... that encourages them to continue pursuing the game' and Claire Connor invokes 'All Stars Cricket for 5 to 8-year-olds [and] the South Asian female activators programme' as concrete examples of steps being taken to attract as wide a range of participants as possible. Danielle Hazell, head coach of Northern Superchargers, talks of how the prominence of the Women's Hundred is a game-changer and umpire, Anna Harris, suggests that 'the more girls who see female umpires, the more it will encourage the mums, sisters and other non-players to give it a go'. There is no shortage of obvious intent when it comes to the overall aim of 'increasing the representation of women' across all aspects of the game.

The optimistic tone and intent of the document doesn't lend itself to grappling with deep-seated problems that bedevil this commitment to inclusivity for girls and women – and the issue is not one confined to cricket. In February 2023, England women's under-23s football team defeated Belgium 4-1 and all 13 players used were white. Head coach Sarina Wiegman acknowledged this as an issue, but, in an echo of Claire Connor's comments, not one that could be solved with a quick fix. 'I don't know how long it will take,' she admitted, but there was an obvious need to find players who 'represent more the diversity of our community'.

A week earlier, the coach of Chelsea women, the massively respected Emma Hayes, had warned of girls' and women's football becoming a middle-class sport as girls from suburban areas were ferried to training grounds by willing parents. She questioned the locating of sporting academies outside the cities and bemoaned the lack of facilities in centrally urban locations. 'Who in their ivory tower has been dreaming up this prawn sandwich girls' football club?' she demanded. This question resonates just as jarringly for those whose sincere intent it is to see greater diversity in cricket. If schools are unable to dedicate time, money and expertise to introducing the game to either boys or girls, and if participation is reliant on parents with time, money and transport to facilitate their children's involvement, how is this pledge to promote equality and diversity going to be honoured? And if it's difficult to do so for a game that has a flagship, successful team that attracts significant TV and live audiences, what's the prospect for a game that lives behind the TV paywall and is tucked away in the corners of the sports pages?

As March 2023 came to a close, two Englishwomen might have merited more space on those pages than they were afforded. In the inaugural final of the Women's IPL, performances of varying quality, but equal impact, from Issy Wong and Nat Sciver-Brunt played a large part in the triumph of the Mumbai Indians franchise. In the eliminator against UP Warriorz, Wong had taken the tournament's first ever hat-trick, picking up the second two wickets by employing the uncomplicated tactic of bowling straight, in the expectation that should the batter miss, the stumps would be knocked over. In the final, she went about her business somewhat differently.

Subscribing to the tried-and-tested maxim from club cricket that filth gets wickets, Wong bowled the second over of the game and her first two full tosses went for ten runs. The third, just below waist height and so a legitimate delivery, resulted in a catch in the deep. This was followed by a dot ball that bounced and was followed up with another full toss deposited into the hands of cover. A final delivery deposited to the boundary finished off a breathless over that went for 2-14. Chasing the 132 for victory, Sciver-Brunt glided to an elegant 60 off 55 to win the game in the final over. Both Wong and Sciver-Brunt were soon to be absent parties to the draft for The Hundred – a process so arcane that clerks from the Byzantine empire would have doubted the complexity of their own processes. Wong was to turn out for Birmingham Phoenix and Sciver-Brunt for the Trent Rockets, but, as important and lucrative as these obligations may have been, as the days lengthened and the weather almost softened, it was the impending Ashes that shimmered on the horizon of English cricket.

Chapter 10

# The Aussies wait in the wings, while cricket lives on in suburb and shire – and maybe even in the city

*To business that we love, we rise betime and go to it with delight.*

Antony: *Antony and Cleopatra*

THE BATS for hire had come home. For the men's Test team, touring obligations from Pakistan to New Zealand, via bolted-on South African and Bangladeshi one-dayers, had been fulfilled. Steve Smith's brief sojourn at Sussex had afforded him the opportunity to settle into English conditions and the jigsaw of the Blast and county cricket continued to bemuse those who wanted to watch some live cricket. The daft 'Test' match against Ireland ran its silly course and Stokesy's boys bundled off to play a bit of golf. And then began the five games against Australia in seven weeks, finishing just before the schools broke up. This year there would be no early autumnal sunshine bathing a wistful Oval as we bid the season goodbye, for this season there was a Hundred to be bashed out under the watchful eye of global franchises eager to gobble up any unclaimed morsels on cricket's table. But another sort of cricket was firmly under way. The ECB estimates that there are some 5,000 assorted cricket clubs in the UK and well before Zak Crawley creamed his first-ball drive along the velvet outfield at Edgbaston, most of them were well into the swing of their season.

When Azeem Rafiq's story found its way to the front and back pages some three years earlier, a number of serious journalists ran features about the enduring popularity of cricket among Britons of Asian heritage and the number of clubs, particularly – but not exclusively – in the north that were sustained by those communities. Among these were the *Guardian*'s Andy Bull, who visited Bowling Old Lane Cricket Club in Bradford in June 2022. He's greeted by a club luminary who is courteously dismissive. 'You're from the *Guardian*? You should just copy and paste the article your paper did when it came here 25 years ago – nothing's changed.' Bull's article highlights the contrast of the 30% of males playing recreational cricket in England of South Asian heritage with the 4% who play professionally. He's an exceptional journalist with impeccable credentials, so it is not intended as disrespect to point out that this is hardly news.

On the Saturday afternoon of the first Test I wander down to the club where I was once first-team captain – an honour quite possibly acquired on account of not paying attention during a routinely dull AGM. A picture on the pavilion wall displays the joint teams from the annual President's game in 1987. There is not one person of colour. Drawn from its north London suburb, the team was a mixture of builders and bankers, taxi drivers and teachers, along with an artist and an agent for professional footballers – the first person I ever saw with a mobile phone. A mixed bunch in terms of income and occupation, but firmly and resolutely white. The contrast between those in the photo and the current team is extraordinary.

To a man they are of South Asian heritage. They range from a few in their late twenties to the majority in their early forties. Disappointingly, there are no 11-year-olds doing a dutiful fielding stint in the hope of taking a blinder or playing out a heroic cameo at number 11. In some ways this is a reflection of a changing local demographic, but in others it is an illustration of cricket's lack of reach into places it once went to find players – with schools being the obvious missing link.

As it happens, I'm saddened that none of my old muckers are around. Had they been, among the gleeful stories with which we entertain ourselves are the fixtures against teams of Afro-Caribbean heritage that once dotted the north London circuit from Haringey to Wood Green to Enfield and beyond. I'll be cautious for fear of accusation of stereotype, but anyone familiar with this level of the game would know that these fixtures produced fiercely competitive cricket, played joyously but with no intention of prisoner capture. Bowling was mainly very fast but, as a consequence, sometimes happily misdirected so that if you hung around long enough, anything that came off the bat raced away for runs. There may have been a dutiful forward defensive when an opponent first came in to bat – often greeted with derisive hoots from the boundary edge – but thereafter, the aim was to hit the ball far, wide and often. In a set-up where grinding out draws when all else was lost was the obvious and acceptable thing to do, such a lily-livered contingency never crossed the mind of these teams. These were games to relish, albeit with a justifiable tinge of fear.

Figures for participation in cricket among the Afro-Caribbean community are now alarmingly low, with around 1% of all recreational players represented. In Chapter 2 we looked at how the supremacy of West Indies cricket was a beacon for Black Britons during the repressive 1980s. Their affiliation to the game had deeply set roots and is well documented. Sport England board director Chris Grant told *The Cricketer* in 2020 that, 'When my father came before Windrush, during the war, cricket was a complete part of his life coming from Jamaica,' before going on to lament that 'Something happened – there was a messy divorce between the Afro-Caribbean community and cricket in England.' In his wonderful evocation of Caribbean voices from the Windrush generation, *Homecoming*, Colin Grant invokes the story of the young boy gifted an improvised cricket bat for his birthday: 'I was four or five. It wasn't a [proper] cricket bat ... but all the boys in our family played cricket.' Bill Morris, who went on to become the first Black leader of a trade union, writes about how he was just about able to tolerate the cold and fog of an unwelcoming Britain because he reckoned he wouldn't be here for long: he'd soon be off home to play for the West Indies. One of Colin Grant's interviewees captured the cultural, as well as the sporting, differences apparent when those from the Caribbean went to watch games. 'You go to Lord's and you see a schoolboy with his father keeping the score, quiet, shh. The West Indians would be commenting on every ball bowled, turning it into more of an event and social occasion ... the crowd wasn't just there to watch – it was a chance to express yourself.'

Should you choose to google a phrase relating to the decline of Afro-Caribbean participation in cricket in the UK, one organisation consistently hits the top of the list: ACE. Launched in January 2020 by Surrey County Cricket Club and operating as a registered charity, ACE has extended its reach to Birmingham and Bristol, with plans to expand to Sheffield, Nottingham and Manchester. Notwithstanding the months rubbed away by Covid, the programme has been relentless in its aim of launching a 'talent search ... designed to engage young people of African and Caribbean heritage' as expressed in its mission statement. With significant funding from Sport England, contributions from the ECB, Royal London and individual donations, ACE's impact has been immediate. Chaired by the charismatic Ebony Rainford-Brent and with consistent backing in the form of lengthy packages from Sky as part of its genuinely committed stance on anti-racism, when it comes to addressing widening participation in cricket, ACE is the biggest player in town.

In January 2023 I set up a meeting with its director, Chevy Green. Our Zoom call is scheduled for an hour, but when, reluctantly, we eventually manage to call it a day, we reckon that we've identified most of the world's cricket problems, even if we don't have instant solutions to them all just yet. It's the first of two conversations over a fortnight, because he invites me to an ACE coaching session at the Oval to see the programme in action and to meet staff, volunteers, participants and parents. He doesn't have to ask twice.

Over the course of these two discussions, he shares his own reminiscences about south London Black cricket. 'The trouble is,' he explains, 'that many of those clubs played on council-owned property and were wandering clubs: when those grounds stopped being maintained, they wandered off and didn't come back.' It's a story I hear repeated in conversation with a group of dads watching their sons – there are some girls training too – going through their paces in the Ken Barrington Cricket Centre. They talk of key individuals moving away from clubs they knew, most frequently just because of age. Along with these 'uncle' figures went energy and input from others, making any continuing identity difficult. Two dads, cousins who have a shared cricketing past in west London, have worked hard to maintain their own local club – 'to make sure our kids have what we had' – and talk of how such contact with the adult world as teenagers taught them lessons about conduct and responsibility as well as cricket. 'And we were a pretty fierce bowling attack,' grins one. We shake hands as we part, his monster hand crushing my feeble fingers, suggesting that he definitely wasn't fibbing.

Other parents reference how their association with local clubs kept their own cricketing interest alive and, as a consequence, their determination to give their children similar opportunities. I am delighted – and marginally surprised – to hear one tell me that his son had been inspired by watching the brilliant *Fire in Babylon* at 13. And just in case that wasn't enough to cement his love of the game, he has met Michael Holding at a Lord's Taverners event, with the great man taking the time and trouble to talk to him about his interest in cricket. Another tells me a similar story about how a meeting with Saqlain Mushtaq through a visit to ACE had left his offspring starstruck and even more determined to succeed.

In the cricket hall, bearing, as it must, the infusion of sweat and boy (despite the presence of a minority of girls) participants ape their heroes, down to the obligatory football warm-up, prior to some vigorous and demanding strengthening and agility routines. There is the obligatory banter adapted for teenage purposes: 'Get bowled out three times and there's no KFC for you.' But there is no doubting the serious intent of every boy and girl as they go about exercises, drills and sequences. They are all aware of the chance they have been afforded and the opportunities that ACE could offer.

Chevy Green is affable, personable and jokey: one of the gang. None of that disguises the firmness of purpose behind ACE. 'I could go to nine primary schools and two secondaries and get everyone involved and give them all a tee-shirt,' he tells me. That is most definitely not what the project is about. 'This is a talent ID programme,' he explains. It's targeted, serious stuff. He knows every boy and girl taking part and, among the older age group, points out those doing their own coaching qualifications, one on a course to become an umpire, another learning the ropes of retail and administration at the Oval. They know they've got the 'golden ticket' by being here; they'd be mad to waste it. Watching them go about their rigorous training, I'm confident they won't.

In the hubbub of the hall, I'm aware of a group forming among the coaches and staff. They're doing what young people do: crowding round someone's phone, laughing along at the contents of a video. After a moment, I realise that the phone-holder and centre of gleeful attention is Ebony Rainford-Brent. She's showing a self-promotional video of herself batting in the nets as well as demonstrating her general fitness. Her default mode is laughter and it infects all around her. She's made the clip, she claims, because the bidding for franchises for the Women's IPL has just got under way and, she proclaims, it's time for her to make a playing comeback and cash in. It's not entirely clear whether or not she's joking.

I catch her attention and before I've really finished my explanation of who I am and why I'm there, she's already got the phone under my nose and asking me what I think. I fudge my answer because I'm still not 100% certain whether she's mucking about. But once we begin talking about ACE and what it has accomplished, we're in full-on serious mode. There are few prompts necessary on my part as she talks proudly but not boastfully about the reach and effect of the programme. Much of what she tells me is a reaffirmation of what I've heard about from Chevy.

I have written earlier about the glib corpo-drivel that infects cricket in the same way that it does so many public and private enterprises. ACE seems to cut through this, demonstrating genuine values and principles being put into action. As I speak to Rainford-Brent, I am reminded of a snippet of a young Black woman coach on one of the Sky videos. 'You can't be what you can't see,' she explains. The clatter and the thumping action in a cricket hall in south London is there to address that invisibility.

Before we finish our conversation, I take the opportunity to tell her how powerful I found her pieces to camera after the murder of George Floyd in Minneapolis in 2020 and the subsequent upsurge of support for Black Lives Matter. I express the view that her anger was palpable as was that of her fellow contributor, Michael Holding. She confirms that the comments were, indeed, born of genuine frustration but that, significantly, ACE had played a huge part in channelling this into something very positive. The next day, by coincidence, I come across further evidence of the impact her organisation is having.

Once again, it's Andy Bull of the *Guardian* who has chosen to look at the game's relationship with race in a piece pre-empting the report of the Independent Commission on Equality in Cricket. Due to be published in 'early 2023', Bull provides a teaser for what promised to be awkward reading for the game's authorities which, eventually, it turned out to be. One significant contributor to the report was Bristol's Mayoral Commission on Race Equality (CORE) – a body clearly not inclined to hold back. 'It is as though the ECB has pulled a lever to lead change across the game on diversity, equality and inclusion,' it observed, 'but the lever isn't actually connected to anything.' There are, though, just a few slivers of light – and of these, the shining star is ACE. CORE's observation that ACE had been instrumental in 'using the wider game to support reconnection with the Black community' would have been as welcome to the dads in a chilly, smelly sports hall as it would to the organisation's high-profile figurehead.

It might have been a touch nippy in the Ken Barrington Centre, but it felt like a caressing breeze from the southern seas in comparison to a chilling Saturday in early May in Luton. Under a sky of unbroken gunmetal and with a biting northerly slicing the air, I go along to watch Luton Caribbean take on Milton Keynes Warriors in Division One of the Four Counties League. I'd made earlier contact with veteran club member Lewis Osborn – Ozzy – and I greet him as he sits tending the scorebook, using his free hand to extract any available warmth from his mug of tea. Luton Caribbean are 52/4 on a pitch that he tells me is sluggish and with a damp, substantial outfield that could have done with the blades being set significantly lower. What does he reckon a decent score to be? Around 130. Some sharpish seam bowling, an injudicious shot or two and, of course, a careless run-out and resultant, vociferous recriminations leave them well short at 92 all out. Their young captain, Adal Bukhari – the run-out victim – is upbeat. 'These got bowled out for 57 last week,' he chirpily informs his shivering team-mates.

Adal, in his early 20s, is one of the longest-serving members of today's team and one of eight players of South Asian heritage. There are just three players with a Caribbean background, with old stager Raphael Barnard dutifully batting at number 11, before sending down a couple of miserly overs in the Warriors' reply. It hasn't always been like this, both he and Ozzy are quick to point out. Founded in 1994, they were one of four Caribbean clubs in the immediate area: they're now the sole survivor, dependent almost entirely on the participation of the South Asian contingent. Talking to them and to the much more youthful Kyron – 'When I tell my mates I play cricket, they think I'm a bit odd' – their explanations are familiar and predictable.

Kyron, whose dad first took him to the club, talks of how cricket wasn't available to him in any meaningful way in his state school. 'It's not a cheap game to play, with all the gear involved,' he tells me, before we talk about the inevitable necessity of parents having to ferry kids to nets and practice as being central to participation. The fact that the game on TV is largely hidden behind the paywall is mentioned by both him and Ozzy as being doubly unhelpful when so many other diversions are so easily accessible. Raphael bemoans the lack of role models from a successful West Indies team, reminiscing fondly of bygone trips to the Oval, only to be queuing five-deep and not getting so much as a glimpse of the action. Our brief conversation is a distillation of pretty well all the issues that have contributed to the diminished tradition of British-based Caribbean cricket.

And it turns out that Adal's cheery optimism has not been misplaced. The Warriors, having also got to 52/4, implode calamitously. Adal himself chips in with three wickets, but, most decisively, three run-outs of varying degrees of incompetence and hilarity contribute to their demise. They slide from 61/4 to 75 all out. The roots of Luton Caribbean may have loosened, but in the surroundings of a neat, if freezing, town cricket club, there exists still the spirit of cricket from a distant time and place.

In warmer surroundings back in February, Sir Andrew Strauss had delivered the MCC Cowdrey lecture to members in the Nursery Pavilion at Lord's. As far as the optics went, there was no brave new equal world on show. Bruce Carnegie-Brown, chair of Marylebone Cricket Club (MCC) (and, oh, chair of Lloyd's of London) introduced proceedings in regulation blazer and MCC tie and congratulated the audience on overcoming the inconvenience imposed by striking rail workers before Strauss took to the stage. Such glimpses of the audience that the recording allowed us revealed no surprises. Listeners are old, white and largely male. While speaking, Strauss doesn't skate far from the safety rail: exciting new era of Stokes and McCullum; a more inclusive game; a recognition of changing times and tastes when it comes to promoting it to new audiences. He acknowledges that cricket needs to be more 'tolerant, understanding, welcoming and embracing of difference.' Dressing room culture needs to change as 'we move forward together as a game with players of different genders, races, creeds and beliefs' which means that 'the traditional macho, hierarchical, perhaps verging on bullying dressing room banter will need to be softened'. Softened but not eradicated. If there's a bull in the Nursery End, Strauss is trying to usher it out rather than grab its horns. When he's finished, Angus Fraser, with no vestige of his status as an international athlete visible to the naked eye, takes to the stage to chair the tamest of discussions with Jonny Bairstow and Tammy Beaumont.

In many ways, the episode is something of a metaphor for how those at the higher echelons of cricket show a lack of genuine appetite for confronting issues of race and class and, possibly, gender. There is recognition that there are problems and that things have to change. There is a willingness to set up committees and investigatory bodies which appears to be laudable. But the tardiness of bodies headed up by the likes of Carnegie-Brown and Strauss, in comparison to the fleet-footedness of Emily Rainford-Brent and ACE, who are literally out on the street finding cricketers, is telling. A keynote lecture headed by a banker, a knight of the realm and a stout ex-pro, all of whom are clearly at their most relaxed once Jonny and Tammy slide into tales of derring-do, is a dispiriting spectacle.

# Chapter 11

# Stokes – the major general for a modern era

*Our doubts are traitors and make us lose the good we oft might win by fearing to attempt.*

Lucio: *Measure for Measure*

THERE IS a telling episode – one among many – towards the end of Luke Mellows and Chris Grubb's insightful and engaging film about Ben Stokes, *Phoenix from the Ashes*.

Throughout the film, renowned director and self-identifying cricket fanatic, Sam Mendes, has been skilfully coaxing as much as he can from the player about his life in the public glare and his extraordinary prowess. Much of this conversation has taken place in a harshly lit, spartan studio, serving to reinforce the gloom that settled on Stokes during the pandemic and the years around it. As the film draws to a close, culminating in the redemption of Stokes's appointment as England Test captain, the location of their conversation moves to airier surroundings.

At Cockermouth Cricket Club, Stokes's boyhood domain, the two men make their way to the wicket. 'Careful,' Stokes grins, 'the groundsman's none too happy.' He serves up a few gentle half-volleys, encouraging Mendes to whack them over the clubhouse – 'I've done it plenty of times as a kid' – and the filmmaker plays straight enough in his brave, but ultimately hopeless, attempts to do so. 'Never put your box in your real underpants,' Mendes cheerily offers as a lame excuse. They retire to the boundary edge and he asks Stokes, with whom it is clear he has formed a trusting relationship, a seemingly simple question. Who does he play cricket for? It's a query he has attempted in a slightly different format earlier in their discussions.

Stokes is flummoxed. And Mendes' attempt to elaborate is of no help to him whatsoever. He tells him that when actors lose direction, he redirects them with a paraphrase of something borrowed from Albert Camus: 'A man's work is nothing but the slow trek to discover, through the detours of art, those two or three great and simple images in whose presence his heart first opened.' The cricketer smiles courteously before telling Mendes that he has 'no idea what you've said'.

It was rumoured that when Mike Brearley successfully captained England during the early 1980s, he collected his thoughts during play by humming snippets of Beethoven. It's an apocryphal story he has never bothered to deny, seemingly revelling in the accepted notion that he brought a cerebral analysis to the game that enabled him to operate on a celestial plane unattainable to the grunts around him. He went on to a career as a psychoanalyst and so he might well have been able to cast the same spell on Stokes as he's supposed to have done on Ian Botham. He'd probably have known his Camus as well as the great composers, but if the high arts are *terra incognita* to England's current Test captain, the sporting world is in no doubt what an act of folly it would be to underestimate the strength of his mind.

'When it gets hard,' explains his friend and predecessor as captain, Joe Root, 'you don't have to turn to him. He turns to you.' His interview appears to be contemporaneous with Mendes' probing of Stokes. Although Root looks less haunted than the blank-eyed, hollowed-out version of Stokes on show, both men bear the marks of months of hotel room isolation and of lives half-lived. When skilfully counterpoised to clips of moments of elation and comradeship on the field of play, this grey-tinged brand of themselves looks particularly poignant. Root's ringing admiration for Stokes's force of personality and extraordinary self-belief casts light on his mate's ability to recover from a hellish range of setbacks.

One of the most frequently replayed cricket clips on YouTube features a wide-eyed Stuart Broad marvelling, along with his colleagues and the Trent Bridge crowd, as Stokes flies off the ground at fifth slip to snatch Adam Voges's airy drive during the 2015 Ashes. As he holds the ball aloft, Stokes points upwards with the claw of an index finger that has caused him constant trouble and pain. This enduring physical nag sits alongside the widely documented and tweeted tribulations that began with the hand fractured punching a locker following a first-ball dismissal in an ODI in Bridgetown in 2014. The incident prompted broadcaster and journalist Mike Selvey to muse that this promising young player might not be the real deal. 'There is genuine reason to believe his mind is not totally on the job and he is in need of a break,' he suggested. To be fair to Selvey, the fully formed player about whom Shane Warne later observed that 'everything he does is flat out – he gets into beast mode', was yet to emerge from the chrysalis.

Once fully installed in the England set-up, three minutes of savagery by Carlos Brathwaite under the lights in Mumbai in 2016 could have turned out to have defined his career. Less than a year later, his late-night brawl in Bristol was beamed to the world and he was omitted from the Ashes squad as a consequence. Whether he was privately gratified to have missed yet another Antipodean mauling is unlikely, given his obvious appetite for a challenge. All these missteps were a world away from the summer of 2019, culminating in a few weeks when he was the force behind England's World Cup victory in July before winning the Headingley Ashes Test on his own.

Days after the final Test in September 2019, during which Stokes had made a relatively low-key contribution to the victory that squared the series but couldn't help retain the Ashes, the *Sun* newspaper chose to run a story deemed by that journal to be in the public interest. In 1988, Stokes's two half-siblings had been murdered by his mother's former husband, who then killed himself. The law, many of whose practitioners will be patrons of the Lord's Long Room, has long filled its coffers by poring over the differences between affairs being in the public interest or of interest to the public. Reviving the 31-year-old case, once fully in the public domain in Stokes's New Zealand homeland, had not infringed the letter of the law. None of which prevented Stokes's mother, Deborah, from invoking the family's stubborn gene and launching legal action. Rather than take on m'learned friends in the public glare, the paper eventually settled for a substantial but undisclosed sum out of court two years later – but not before its damage had been well and truly done.

Superficially, Stokes seemed angry but unaffected. At the start of 2020, he bloody-mindedly ensured that England won in Cape Town for the first time since 1957 by flogging himself into a 90mph spell at the end of the fifth day when all around him had flagged. At about the same time, his father, Gerard, was diagnosed with the brain cancer that killed him by the end of the year ... and, of course, the world peered ignorantly at the brink of the Covid abyss.

Cricket did its level best to provide some sort of spectacle as the restrictions of the first lockdown were gradually eased during the summer of 2020. Teams from the West Indies and Pakistan undertook tours of England, the reciprocation for which turned out to be flaky in the extreme, but some decent games were played out for subscription TV and its paying punters. In the series against the West Indies, Stokes played a significant part with bat and ball before a dismal and distracted performance in the first game against Pakistan presaged his withdrawal from the squad. The whirlpool of the succeeding months' schedule, during which his father died at the end of 2020, sucked him into a ghastly vortex.

It would be unfair to put all the blame on cricket's authorities for its fevered attempts to bring some normality and diversion to unprecedented and challenging times. The game's mistakes in this regard were minimal in comparison to the misjudgement of a political class whose venal, self-serving approach to crisis resulted in widespread corruption and cronyism, the extent of which has yet to be fully revealed. Long before it emerged that the lawmakers were so blinded by entitlement that they had genuinely convinced themselves that rules were just for the little people, they'd already cooked up the loony-tune plan of herding people into restaurants so that new variants of the disease could happily incubate and multiply. Against this background, to expect the ECB to operate in a manner that showed perception and courage, especially in a way that might affect its already echoing coffers, would be the genuine triumph of hope over experience.

With society still unsure whether it was permissible to have a cup of tea with grandma in the garden, cricket asked its senior players – now trudging from hotel room to nets, on to the field of play and then dining at separate tables before settling into their rooms again – to undertake a schedule specifically designed to sap and snap them. Once the Pakistan series concluded in the late summer of 2020, a bolt-on set of ODIs and T20s took place against Australia. I know I've made the point earlier, but a small prize goes to anyone who could tell me the outcome of any of these games. These were followed by an aborted visit to South Africa where, after three T20s, the planned ODIs were cancelled as the virus spread for another wave. As the new year dawned, England went out to more deserted grounds in Sri Lanka for two Joe Root benefit matches resulting in England victories – but not before they recovered from 29/3 to knock off the 74 needed to win in the first of these.

Stokes, unlike England fan Rob Lewis, who kept a solitary vigil from the fort at Galle throughout, gave Sri Lanka a miss, but travelled out for the marathon in India which followed. Four Test matches took place behind closed doors but, for the first time since the 2005 Ashes, were covered by terrestrial TV in the UK – touchingly by Channel 4, whose coverage had contributed so significantly to the profile of that seminal series. These gruelling encounters were followed by five T20s and three ODIs. The first two T20s were played in front of delighted crowds of over

66,000 in Ahmedabad, most of whom seemed to think that mask-wearing was so last year. Thereafter, restrictions were reimposed as infections in the area spiked. England returned home for a couple of undistinguished Tests against New Zealand in June before a whole bunch of T20s and ODIs against Sri Lanka prior to another batch of the same against Pakistan.

Eventually, the tab had to be picked up. On 30 July 2021, the ECB announced that 'Ben Stokes, the talismanic England all-rounder, is taking an indefinite break from all cricket in order to prioritise his mental wellbeing.' The issue of the injured finger which had never properly healed was also invoked, but there was no doubting the significance of the identification of mental health issues from England's Superman. Just for context, and even allowing for a degree of player rotation, in the 13 months prior to this announcement, England's men had played 14 Test matches, 15 ODIs and 15 T20s. A further five-Test series against India was to follow – albeit only four of these were completed in 2021. All of these playing commitments were fulfilled while living in bubble conditions. For Stokes, this whirlwind was compounded by not being with his father during his final weeks – an issue which he only openly acknowledged in retrospect and which he told the *Telegraph* had made him 'hate cricket' and admit that he 'should have opened up about it sooner'. If there was an awful inevitability about his openness and his condition, it didn't prevent the shock and surprise that accompanied it.

In *Phoenix from the Ashes*, when talking of the fallout for Stokes from his openness, Jos Buttler muses that the collective wisdom is that 'if anyone can handle it, it'd be Ben'. Joe Root talks of how his mate is 'perceived as invincible'. These are revealing observations. Almost at the very moment when the heroic figure reveals doubt and weakness, deeply entrenched notions of inner strength are invoked as qualities that will prevail and enable him to overcome. Even allowing for the intention of Mendes' film to combine music and image to manipulate emotion, watching the unalloyed zeal of Stokes's solitary rehab and training leaves the viewer in complete awe of his single-mindedness and self-belief. Stokes may well be bemused by Camus, but it is impossible to imagine a mind more intense and focused. So focused, in fact, that by the end of October 2021, he announced himself fit and ready for the winter in Australia. He did so by posting the message that he was 'ready for Australia' on his Twitter account, along with a picture of the urn. Subsequent events suggested that a hanky tied to a stick might have been a more suitable image.

By the time Ollie Robinson ran to square leg to allow Pat Cummins to clean bowl him on a chilly Hobart evening in January 2022, Stokes, along with everyone involved in English cricket, was probably watching from behind the nearest sofa. His own meagre contribution to the series had amounted to 236 runs scored across ten completed innings, along with four wickets at a touch over a pricey 71. Not that it would ever have crossed his mind to do so, but he could have argued that with just one century and two five-wickets hauls by Englishmen across the series, he was hardly lagging behind high-achieving colleagues.

Eleven years earlier, on 7 January 2011, the cruellest and most cacophonous away following ever installed at the Sydney Cricket Ground shook the roof as Chris Tremlett's first ball to Mitchell Johnson took out his middle stump. Later in the day, the innings victory was completed, the Ashes duly retained and the series won. In the dozen years since, there have been no England victories and almost nothing approaching an even contest on Australian soil. One of the wearily predictable consequences of this is a perfectly justifiable combination of hand-wringing and navel-gazing on the part of those who run the English game. This starts way before the players are even on the plane home. His own dander having risen to audible proportions as he commentated on the final few moments in Hobart, Jonathan Agnew told *Wisden* magazine that, 'We must wake up to the fact that if our first-class game is not fit for purpose, then England will not have any Test cricketers.' His was just one voice in the chorus of despair and frustration.

It speaks to either the utter loyalty or complete obtuseness of then CEO of English cricket, Tom Harrison, that he managed, with a completely straight face, to suggest that the Ashes defeat was a 'brilliant opportunity' to 'reset and recalibrate' the domestic game. Since that heady day in 2011, England's men have played 15 Tests in Australia, lost 13 of them, scraping the squeakiest of draws in one and plodding through a rain-affected nonentity in the other. Harrison doubled down on the corpo-speak and pledged his trust in the 'fantastic' Joe Root as captain. It wasn't quite his last act as head of the ECB, but by the time the clocks had gone forward and the county season had made its usual four-seasons-in-a-day faltering start, Harrison was plying his trade with Six Nations rugby and Stokes was making ready to complete the turnaround from locker-punching, nightclub-brawling, streetfighter cricketer to getting his portrait up there with C.B. Fry, Douglas Jardine and Len Hutton.

England's newly installed manager of England men's cricket, Rob Key, had little doubt about the value of the appointment. 'He epitomises the mentality and approach we want to take this team forward into the next era of red-ball cricket,' he explained. In the English summer of 2022, as Stokes insisted on putting the overall performance of the team above all individual stats and performances – including, most noticeably, his own – Key would have been happily relaxed about his decision. Events during the Tests against New Zealand, India, South Africa and Pakistan demonstrated that the commitment to a very different form of five-day cricket was no flash in the pan. Stokes himself displayed a bone-headed determination to subjugate self to team with occasional recklessness with the bat and the self-flagellation of overlong bowling spells. In doing so, the words spoken about him by Shane Warne during Sam Mendes' film ring clear and true. 'Ask any fan around the world,' he suggested, 'about any player and what they average and they wouldn't have a clue – but they'll remember how they played the game.'

By the spring of 2023, Stokes would have been hoping that Warne's words were being heeded by those looking to him to justify his £1.6m contract with Chennai Super Kings. Two single-figure knocks and an over slapped for 18 wasn't looking like a good return for the franchise – and that was before an injured toe curtailed his participation in the early part of the tournament. His enforced absence allowed time for Sky Sports to interview him with the garish razzmatazz of contemporary cricket crashing around behind him. He knew what his best side would be for Australia and his preference for 'fast, flat wickets' was a priority, even if that might suit some opposition batters. The prime requirements were to 'score quickly' and, if possible, 'having the option to bowl above 90mph'. Would he offer a tempting declaration if England were 2-1 up on the final day and there was the possibility of a result? Of course he would. 'I'm not going to change anything just because we're in the Ashes ... I [wouldn't be] being true to myself and everything I've done this past year.'

Meanwhile, in contrast to the sweaty glow of the Chepauk Stadium, cricket made its multi-sweatered foray out of English dressing rooms. Depending on conditions, batters tried to stock up on cheap early season runs on offer from creaky seamers, while a few of those same trundlers did the April thing of putting it on a length and letting nature do the rest. Whether England's Test captain was paying any attention in the light of his predetermined team selection is impossible to know. Similarly, only he will know the extent to which he took note of another of cricket's spring rituals.

In mid-April, the 160th edition of *Wisden* was published – creeping close to a hefty £60 per copy. For the third time in four years, Stokes was named as Leading Cricketer in the World. 'It is hard to think of any other cricketer who could have transformed his team's fortunes so suddenly as Ben Stokes,' wrote editor, Lawrence Booth. And, indeed, it seems impossible to do so. Almost. Because it all depends on what you mean by cricket team.

Stokes's contribution to the energy and joy that Test cricket has generated in England is enormous. There were obvious signs that this vigour had communicated itself, in part, away from England to crowds in Pakistan and New Zealand. The player is not on record anywhere about assuming the mantle of the saviour of the Test match form, but it's not fanciful to suggest that this is a role that some may see as being ascribed, albeit unwittingly, to him. One thing is for certain: if Stokes – along with McCullum – is instrumental in keeping the longest form of the game alive, they are doing so against huge odds, swimming against the tide of voracious franchises backed by huge media corporations. For the sake of their health, county members might do best not to fret over the spectre of nation states such as Saudi Arabia, eager to expand their sportswashing empires, creeping and hovering in the shadows.

Lawrence Booth, a hugely influential voice in the English game, does not shy away from the enormity of the situation. Concluding his *Wisden* editorial, he speculates about the very nature of the game as a spectator sport. 'Three power blocs are in a relationship that is part-symbiotic, part-parasitic,' he suggests. 'The T20 franchises, in it for themselves; the ICC, nominally in charge; and the national boards, keen to placate broadcasters and generate their own revenue.' The strength of mind of Stokes and his Cool Hand Luke of a partner are irrefutable. Their accomplishments in the year prior to the 2023 Ashes had been as influential as they'd been rollickingly enjoyable. But as Steve Smith had his first squint at the nets in Hove, both of them would have known that the events of the next few months could define their contribution to the game in a way that went significantly beyond just another Ashes series. As the status of Test cricket diminished ineluctably towards the Anglo-Australian-Indian axis, the 2023 Ashes assumed ever more significance for the way top-level cricket would be played, watched and paid for.

*Wisden* may have been on the bookshelves; those so inclined may have been getting their cricket fix from the slogfest of the IPL; the rug and thermos brigade might even have chanced an afternoon at the county ground. But as the seasons just about changed, cricket rarely made it to the sports pages. Which wasn't to say that it was absent from the news. At the end of March, the Cricket Disciplinary

Committee ruled that it was not satisfied that 'on the balance of probabilities' Michael Vaughan had made comments that could be construed as racist to players of South Asian origin prior to a game in 2009. The same body was clear in its judgement that this conclusion did 'not in any way undermine the wider assertions made by Azeem Rafiq' about institutional racism within the game. With Vaughan himself expressing discontent with the conduct of proceedings and with others so accused still refusing to attend, the episode ended with the mess and fudge so consistent with how English cricket runs its affairs. 'There are no winners in [this] process,' Vaughan observed. It may have been a cliché, but it rang true enough.

On the release of the findings, Rafiq gave an almost instant interview to Sky News from his new home in Dubai. In a polished and relaxed set of responses, he talked with unswerving certainty about how, despite being the catalyst for the row about cricket's institutional racism, there was now a need for reconciliation and a willingness from all parties to confront those issues which had 'cost me my career'. It was not about individuals; it was about healing time; there was a need to get into a room together. If the interview had something of the feel of a convert to cod psychology parroting the phrases of an earnest counsellor, one would hope that even the most vehement of Rafiq's critics would have the grace to cut him some slack. He now sees himself in the role of standard bearer for equality in cricket. A few days prior to the CDC ruling, he had told an event organised by the *i* newspaper that he was 'incredibly determined to make sure other people's lives change, other people get opportunities, fair opportunities ... that's what I get out of bed for now'. He talked of how he felt a sense of responsibility which tied in with his faith: 'I feel like I've been handed a responsibility from Allah.'

And still, somewhere lodged in the admirative labyrinth, the Independent Commission into Equality in Cricket report was trying to blink itself into the light of day. Due to report in 'early 2023' and with its website closed to submissions for months, its chair, Cindy Butts, was on record talking about the staggering volume of response. As Stokes nursed his toe in Chennai and Baz started looking out the cones, bibs and practice balls, cricket's administrators were singularly failing to take their cue from the fearless dynamism that was driving those at the top of its playing pyramid. The pen-pushers were hoping, no doubt, that the exploits of the world's best cricketer and those around him, on to whom he would sprinkle his magic dust, would keep them out of the spotlight. For the man himself, their delay, obfuscation and timidity were worlds away from his immediate, single-minded ambitions.

## Chapter 12

# The Ashes 2023.
# Cricket providing its own
# best advert for itself

*Then with the losers sympathise, for*
*nothing can seem foul to those that win*

King Henry IV: *Henry IV part i*

IT APPEARS to be mandatory that TV coverage of Test cricket in England includes a swoop around the fizz-drinkers in the posh boxes. Tim Rice, Mick Jagger, John Major ... you know the drill. Cue the usual clichés about how the wonderful game brings together such disparate characters. At such times, the portly, patrician figure of Stephen Fry seems to muscle his way into most of these tableaux of the privileged. At the start of May 2023, he had handed the presidency of MCC to the equally clubbable Mark Nicholas, feted by Fry as someone 'as deeply steeped in cricket as anyone I know'.

During his Cowdrey Lecture to the club in November 2021, Fry had demonstrated acute awareness of the issues facing the game in terms of race and class. Speaking of how 'relatively easy it has been for people like me to afford membership of this club', he went on to develop the argument that such an advantaged existence was in stark contrast to those whose access to the game was constrained by issues of class and race. A few weeks after bequeathing his badge of office, he was to be heard on BBC's *Broadcasting House* gushing about Bazball while expressing the usual concern for the future of the longest form of the game. He'd been caught on camera at Lord's the day before, watching England being held up by stubborn Irish resistance. As a curtain-raiser for the summer's main event, the game hadn't been much of an advert.

Given his concerns expressed in the Cowdrey lecture, Fry may have noted that of the 22 players who lined up prior to the start of the game, there was not one person of colour. By contrast, when the same national football teams had last played each other in November 2020, there were eight: five in England's starting XI and three in Ireland's. There were other absences. Missing from Ireland's team was Josh Little, easily their most accomplished bowler. In discussion with Cricket Ireland (CI), it had been agreed that Little would rest up after his exertions with Gujarat Titans, defeated IPL finalists. CI's performance director, Richard Holdsworth, raised eyebrows, and probably a few hackles, by announcing that although playing a Test at Lord's was a special occasion, it was 'not a pinnacle event – and where we have to put our energies and ensure we have the best team on the park is in our pinnacle events'. In this case, these were the forthcoming qualifiers for the ODI World Cup in the autumn.

Holdsworth also referenced the fact that with almost no red-ball cricket behind him, Little may have struggled to meet the demands of a five-day Test match – although with

Bazball and the gruesome mismatch between the teams, he couldn't have seriously contemplated the game lasting anything like that long. More pragmatically, Little probably felt he needed to be spared the leather-chasing that his colleagues endured at the home of cricket. Since the last day of March, he'd played ten games for the Titans, breaking off to play for Ireland in three ODIs in Bangladesh. In all, he'd bowled 62 overs in 60 days. He'd earned just short of half a million pounds from his spell with the Titans, seven times more than his central contract with CI. His Irish employers may have been helpful with the spin put on his decision, but it's unlikely that there'd been too much agonising going on in the Little household.

Nonetheless, by the time Ireland had lost the first of their three World Cup qualifiers before the end of June, there may have been some rueful head-shaking from Holdsworth and the bowler himself. A surprise defeat to Oman, followed by a last-ball thriller against Scotland, left them needing to beat Sri Lanka to have a chance of progressing. By the time Dimuth Karunaratne had guided his team to a total of 325 with a run-a-ball century, Little's eight overs had cost him 78 with no reward. By that point, his tournament figures of 4-198 from 28 overs suggested that an outing at Lord's might not have been such a bad idea after all.

Once England had sauntered through their extended net, a proper cricket match took place across the Thames at the Oval. Australia looked swaggeringly ominous as they breezed past India and their rumbustious support to win the World Test Championship. Accumulating over 700 runs in two innings at a respectable rate of 3.5 an over, and then capturing 20 Indian wickets while giving their pace attack 113 demanding overs, looked like pretty decent preparation for the big show. Well over half of those runs were scored by the solid-looking middle order of Marnus Labuschagne, Steve Smith and Travis Head, only one of whom, cricket's Mr Fidget, had been earning his crore down in the IPL. Head was unsold at auction and Labuschagne had made a lifestyle decision not to participate. 'If money is the driver and people can see that they can earn more playing white-ball rather than Test cricket,' he told the *Guardian*'s Simon Brunton, 'then people are going to take that route ... but I certainly don't think that's going to be for everyone.'

It's an attitude shared by his team-mate, Mitchell Starc. Talking of involvement in franchise cricket as 'the fast track to notoriety', Starc, whose contract with Cricket Australia is, admittedly, one of the plumper on offer, adopts a wider perspective of his place in the game. 'Over a hundred years of Test cricket,' he told Andy Bull of the same newspaper, 'and there's been less than 500 men who have played it for Australia – that in itself makes it very special to be a part of it.' With his wife, Alyssa Healy, the captain of Australia's women gearing up for an equally demanding summer, his invocation of the cliché of spending quality time with family rang especially true.

Once Manchester City and its Gulf sponsor had cemented their domination of world, nay interplanetary, football, cricket eventually found some space to nudge its way into the sports news. As the forthcoming concertinaed Ashes worked their way up the agenda, the loss of Jack Leach was treated as a minor catastrophe in the making, Stokes's non-bowling appearance against Ireland ratcheted up speculation about his role as an all-rounder and his pulling up following the taking of a routine catch prompted wilder speculation about his ability to play five Test matches over the course of 45 days – although he was hardly on his own when it came to the prospect of fulfilling this bizarre outcome of the great cricketing calendar catastrophe. It was all reassuringly familiar: where will we find a spinner; what about the all-rounder spot; how flimsy is the middle order; which quick will break down first? As a build-up to the theatre of the Ashes, it was conforming to the script to the letter. That is, until an unruly audience member created an unwelcome disturbance.

On Monday, 12 June, two very different media interviews took place. On Radio 5, the newly recalled Moeen Ali happily admitted that he was never going to be a like-for-like replacement for Jack Leach. 'I've never been able to hold an end up,' he admitted, 'and when I have, it's because I've been taking wickets ... I've hardly ever bowled for England where I've thought I need to go at two an over.' His selection was, in his opinion, 'a free hit' and, in an astonishingly counterintuitive comment, he talked of a lack of pressure to do well. 'I spoke to Baz, and he's not bothered about how I perform, which is quite nice.' The well-documented difference between McCullum's outward insouciance and his fervid attention to detail once behind doors, suggests that Mo may well have been underplaying the message.

But if Moeen's self-deprecation might have made the back page, it was Colin Graves's interview with Sky News earlier in the day that restored cricket to the main news coverage. The former chair of Yorkshire still seemed to be feeling sore about his removal. In 2002, he had used the Graves Family Trust to bail out the club to the tune of nearly £15m. Possibly miffed by the slow rate of repayment, he had made a bid to return to his former position, prompting speculation that, in doing so, he would oversee the sale of the club to buyers of his choice. His grab for power was, however, short-lived – but that didn't stop him from, as he probably saw it, taking a few prisoners with him. If disapproval of banter and discriminatory languages had eventually made its way into cricket's overall consciousness, most of this progress had passed Mr Graves by.

His protestations had a weary staleness about them. Even if true – 'I can tell you now, nothing was brought up in the club, nothing on the table about racism allegations whatsoever' – the fact that Graves seemed unaware of how inappropriately lame such a defence sounded speaks volumes about his obtuseness. If he'd stopped there it would have been just plain bad: it didn't and it got worse. He went on to explain that he thought there had 'been odd occasions where words have been said that people may regret afterwards'. This was not 'done on a racist, savage basis. I think there was a lot of – I know people don't like the word banter – but I think there could have been a lot of banter in there about it, and I know people don't like that.'

In the three years since Rafiq's first allegations, one would have imagined that anyone associated with cricket or, indeed, any sport, whose antennae were not sufficiently calibrated to vibrate uncontrollably at the use of the term 'banter', had clearly been walking around with their head in close proximity to their fundament. Such nuance had passed Graves by, but the radar of cricket's general overlords was bleeping within seconds of his interview. Having dissociated themselves from his comments and expressing the view that racist views must never again become normalised, the ECB went on to say that 'we vehemently disagree that this is "just banter" and believe that any debate in that regard should stop immediately. Racism isn't banter.'

Those same authorities probably waited as impatiently as anyone for the action to begin on the Friday after Graves's remarks. As it turned out, they would have been as relieved as they were delighted that what happened once the games commenced became the best gravedigger of bad news that English cricket could ever have hoped for. Between 16 June and 31 July, England's cricketers, men and women alike, were participants in utterly captivating contests that did exactly what sport should do: divert, distract and entertain. And given the state of a burning world, with the poor getting ever poorer and populists turning the global clock back on democracy, cricket did its level best to lighten the mood – even though the TV paywall, with a couple of brief exceptions, stayed firmly in place.

One exception to the monopoly imposed by Sky and Now TV was the first T20 in the women's Ashes, for which the BBC had joint rights. Having lost the only Test – worth four points as opposed to two for the shorter games – in the multi-format series, England were faced with the formidable prospect of beating the visitors five times out of six over the shorter formats. Given Australia's utter dominance in limited-overs games, such a turnaround looked highly unlikely. Once the visitors reached the required 154 in front of nearly 20,000 spectators in a genuine thriller at Edgbaston – where else? – in the first T20, they were 6-0 up with a further 10 points to play for. One more win from five games would mean that they couldn't be overtaken and, as holders of the Ashes, would retain the trophy. Two victories would mean taking the series outright.

England's Amy Jones dutifully told the media after the Edgbaston game that the team had 'felt like underdogs the whole way through, but it feels to us as if the gap is closing and that's a really exciting feeling'. And it turned out that this wasn't just the required repetition of the positivity mantra, by now the established hallmark of both England's men's and women's teams. Over the next eight days, England won three games on the bounce. With victories at the Oval and at Lord's – again, in front of crowds of over 20,000 on both occasions – they inflicted the first T20 series defeat on Australia for six years. Four days after Alice Capsey's thunderous 46 off 23 balls ensured the DLS win in south London, England successfully chased down 264 to win the first ODI in Bristol, to level the series at six points all. Capsey, whose opening stand of 84 from 10 overs with Tammy Beaumont set the base from which England stuttered but were then guided home by the calm dependability of Heather Knight, repeated the article of faith. 'Going into this we were the underdogs,' she told the press. 'To get over the line, especially in pressure moments … [it] has been brilliant to fight back and put pressure on the Aussies.'

The next stage of that fightback took place during the lull in the breathless men's series on 16 July at the Ageas Bowl in Southampton. The venue's website cheekily suggested that the game was a sellout while talking of how the 'England Women will be roared on by 12,000 spectators', which is something below its permanent capacity of 15,000 which rises to 25,000 for 'bigger matches'. On a glorious afternoon in between the downpours of July, Australia, batting first, were 256/9 with one over remaining. Georgia Wareham then proceeded to bludgeon 26 from the normally reliable Lauren Bell, setting a target that looked significantly more challenging than had seemed likely five minutes earlier. At 203/7, 80 short with just over 11 overs remaining, England looked out of the game. And so, just about, it turned out, but not before Nat Sciver-Brunt, ably assisted by Sarah Glenn, batted with skill and nerve, leaving herself needing to hit the last ball for six for a victory or four for a super over. A leg-side heave never looked like getting to the boundary and so, at 8-6 up, Australia retained the Ashes.

Almost predictably, during those 45 days during which cricket furnished proof that sport is, indeed, the greatest unscripted drama, England went to Taunton and, belying the close nature of previous encounters, brushed aside their opponents, thereby winning both short-form competitions and squaring the series, although not regaining the Ashes. Nat Sciver-Brunt's 129, along with 67 from her skipper, enabled the hosts to post 285/9, a score which the visitors never looked like threatening. 'There's disappointment we haven't got the Ashes,' said Knight, 'but it's a draw, and if you'd told me that at 6-0 down, I would have bitten your hand off.'

Knight declared herself 'super proud' of what her team had achieved and over at the ECB, they were feeling pretty chipper as well. Revelling in the sale of over 94,000 tickets for the multi-format series – nearly three times as many as in 2019 – the board's CEO, Richard Gould, talked of 'a landmark moment and ... yet more evidence of the growing momentum behind the women's game'. Looking around the crowds at all the games, Gould's optimism could seem justified. Family groups with plenty of girls and women; sets of mates that were not exclusively male boozing companions; good-natured, raucous support devoid of some of the late-evening boorishness of the men's game. Plenty to be pleased with.

But as to whether England's women really were to be the poster girls of a game for everyone – the We Got Game that was the chosen brand name for the women's Ashes – remains open to question. Of the 11 women who played in the series-leveller at Taunton, there was one person of colour. Six of the team were privately educated. All had been put in contact with cricket club networks that had supported their development; in terms of social capital, they are all, indisputably, advantaged. The report of the Independent Commission for Equity in Cricket (ICEC), which we'll look at in detail in the final chapter, had eventually delivered its stark message that 'cricket is not a game for everyone' at just about the same time that Tammy Beaumont was becoming the first Englishwoman to score a double hundred in a Test match. Gould and his colleagues might have enjoyed the warm glow of success but would have known that deep-seated problems of equality and access were a demanding work in progress.

They could have been pardoned, however, for sliding the tricky jobs to the bottom of the in-tray while, for 45 days, the glorious spectacle of Test cricket showcased the utter magnificence of the product they were there to promote. Earlier in this book, I referenced the notion that even the most committed follower of England cricket would be hard-pressed to recall the outcomes of many bi/tri-lateral one-day series. I venture to suggest that those same aficionados will have no such trouble when it comes to remembering, in some detail, each of the five Ashes Tests of 2023. A measure of the nature of the four games with a positive outcome comes from the Association of Cricket Statisticians. You may have already formed a mental picture of the composition of this body and, should you go to their website, a screenshot of their Zoom AGM may not come as huge surprise to you. These bearded wonders define a close finish in a five-day game as one that is won by fewer than three wickets or 50 runs. By these criteria, all four results were, indeed, close finishes. But then my last guess is that if you're reading this book, you didn't need anyone to tell you that.

Whether those in the England camp liked it or not, Bazball became the buzzword for the entire series. If McCullum thought it an irksome label from the start, he, like everyone else, might have become slightly dazed and confused as to what it was by the time the teams trooped amiably from the Oval on the last day of July. Coined originally as a joke by *Cricinfo* journalist, Andrew Miller, Google searches now pull up over eight million results for the term. I know I couldn't have been alone in being asked by non-cricket-loving acquaintances what it meant. My shorthand response was that it is the elimination of the fear of failure; taking the bold and positive decision rather than opting for safety first. It manifests itself in a refusal to be cowed, a determination to stand by your decisions and your team-mates. Predictably, it ruffles feathers; it challenges accepted truisms. When it fails, it pisses some people off. In the spirit of full disclosure, I'm not one of them.

Two player interviews perfectly captured this bold, unapologetic mindset. Unremorseful aggression was now the default position. At the end of the second day's play at Lord's, the BBC's Jonathan Agnew was left in no doubt that this was the case. Addressing Australia's total of 416, the new world order of Crawley, Pope and Duckett had got England to 188/1 after 38 overs. Seven overs later, they were 222/4, with Pope, Root and Duckett, on 98, all out caught playing pull shots. During that period, Nathan Lyon pulled up with an injury that looked – as it was – certain to keep him out of the rest of the game. 'What about the general mood in the dressing room,' Aggers asked Duckett, about the fact that 'three front-line batsmen get out in that fashion ... and with the spinner off the field injured?'

A rueful shake of the head over a chance to be on the honours board? A grudging acceptance that maybe things hadn't gone quite as they'd wished? Not in this New England. 'I'm not sure how to answer that,' Duckett replied, going on to say that he was 'surprised about the question ... we've played positive cricket for the past 12 months and we're certainly not going to change. We're very happy with the position we're in. If we can eke closer to them and even get a lead, I think we're on top in this game.' Sorry to miss out on a century at Lord's? Kinda. 'Ten metres either side of him there and I've got a hundred ... it's a shot I play and it's a shot I've scored plenty of runs [with] so I'm not happy I got out, but I'd rather get out like that.'

If Duckett's demeanour in his interview with Agnew and other media had the air of a bemused, recalcitrant schoolboy, there was nothing remotely subtle about Jonny Bairstow's outspoken responses to Sky's Ian Ward at Old Trafford following his 99 not out from 81 balls to take England just shy of 600. The player had been living in interesting times.

The second day of the first Test at Edgbaston was his nadir. Having batted well the previous day to score a run-a-ball 78, the most untrained of eyes could detect that he was not at his mobile best when behind the stumps. During the afternoon and evening he became a special beneficiary to a player to whom Fate was soon to bind him in the most notorious of ways. With Australia at 220/4, Moeen got through the defences of Cameron Green, bringing Bairstow's opposite number to the wicket. Deciding that the English spinner needed taking down, Alex Carey did a little dance down the track and missed, leaving Bairstow with a simple stumping. Which he fluffed with all the inelegance of a one-armed juggler. His woes did not end there.

With Carey on 26, he dropped a regulation chance from a perfect Root off break and then temporarily denied Jimmy Anderson one of his few successes in the series by dropping him again when he was on 52. He was unable to perform any further biffing heroics with the bat until Manchester and, at times, looked a sorry, flailing figure. He earned the happy plaudits of the MCC gentry by carting off that crusty protester, who was one of those miseries out to spoil people's fun, and then he prompted their righteous indignation by being a dopey clot. But he looked like a man carrying the mark of failure. The spectre of Ben Foakes, who became a better player with every day of his absence, hovered over everything he did.

When he came out to join Harry Brook on that teasingly sunny afternoon at Old Trafford with England on 437/5, the stage was set and he didn't disappoint. As Pat Cummins resorted to the familiar ploy of ringing the boundary with fielders, Jonny blasted and bludgeoned into the spaces and over the ropes. In a last-wicket stand of 66 with Anderson, the bowler contributed just 5. With Australia four down at the close and on the brink of a defeat that didn't materialise as the monsoon set in, it was time to face the cameras. He stayed on the front foot.

To the popular media notion that he performed better when criticised, he responded: 'It gets a bit tiresome to be honest with you.' Had he suffered from insufficient preparation? 'The surgeon says, "I'm surprised you're walking and running, never mind playing professional sport" – I'm delighted to be where I am.' On Bazball: 'That's exactly how we've played our cricket ever since Ben came in charge of the side and that's what we're sticking by.' On the media: 'They can say what they want … they're paid to have an opinion … if they don't have an opinion, they don't have a job.'

He remained coyly evasive about the stumping at Lord's; others had been less temperate. Australian prime minister, Anthony Albanese, had already spotted the Ashes as a handy distraction from politics as usual, hailing Cummins as a 'national hero' after the Edgbaston game and calling it 'one of the greatest Test matches of all time'. Perhaps in a nod to these new, chummier times, he conceded that England had played with 'courage and conviction,' showing 'the sort of spirit and sportsmanship which their team is certainly known for'. This emollient tone soon faded. When Rishi Sunak expressed the view that 'he wouldn't want to win a game in the manner that Australia did', Albanese tweeted his advice that his counterpart should remember what they were both taught as schoolboys and 'stay in his crease'. He went on to 'wish the PM well' in an effort, perhaps, to maintain some sort of perspective and goodwill.

His minister for the republic, Matt Thistlethwaite, took a harsher line. 'If you ever want an illustration of why Australia should become a republic,' he tweeted, 'it's a frothing and possibly pickled member of the MCC targeting Usman Khawaja in the Long Room at Lord's. Old Britain reminding Australia of our place.' MCC acted quickly to suspend three members and offered an unreserved apology to the Australian team. Andrew Strauss who, along with most professional opinion, dubbed Bairstow's actions dozy, was widely quoted as saying that the rumbustious crowd behaviour following the dismissal was attributable to 'people who don't normally come to Lord's', although I have yet to find a reliable source confirming this. The overarching narrative was that this was all justifiable behaviour because the Australians had infringed 'the spirit of cricket'.

Really? Honestly? Wherein, precisely, do those that resort to this tired old cliché think this spirit resides? Is it at Lord's itself, with every inch of space, within and beyond the playing perimeter, monetised and sloganised up to the hilt? Is it about membership of MCC, for which a wait of up to two decades, personalised invitations and selective interviews are required? Is it in the game's governing bodies that signally fail, year after year, to put together a coherent calendar of fixtures? Or in a game that fails to tap into talent because much of it is located in clubs and communities beyond leafy shires? Or in boardrooms where some people think that, really and truly, this racism stuff is just old-fashioned banter?

Or does this spirit mean that it's just the luck of the draw if you get four (or should that have been three?) controversial overthrows to win a World Cup? Or a change of ball at 140/0 followed by ten wickets for fewer than 200 on a flat deck? Or does it simply boil down to quick thinking by our chaps as opposed to sharp practice by Johnny Foreigner?

Bairstow, the Long Room, Sunak and Albanese – as well as the brilliance of the matches themselves – all succeeded in putting English Test cricket on the front pages. By the time of the evening news on all UK TV channels on 31 July, with plenty going on in the world, England's victory to level the series was the headline. The same had been true on the Sunday evening when, in the aftermath of Mark Wood and Chris Woakes guiding England through the most jangling of afternoons, England had prevailed at Headingley. 'England's Ashes are alive,' panted Nasser Hussain as Woakes hit the winning boundary. 'Test cricket is alive.' In the glorious aftermaths of that victory and the one at the Oval, and even in tight defeat, it certainly felt like it. The euphoria of victory doesn't exist to be tarnished by harsh analysis.

It is Mike Atherton who takes to the microphone at the Oval to interview the England captain, whose post-match interviews become increasingly Zen as time moves on. Yes, Stokes agrees, it is about making memories. He is aware of his responsibility for the longest form of the game. It has been a series where he 'genuinely feel[s] it's almost what Test cricket needed'. What's more, his colleagues agree. 'Every player is a massive advocate for Test cricket and wants [it] to stay alive,' he tells Atherton. Any loss of appetite? Is he looking forward to India in the winter? 'It's very hard to lose your appetite when you love Test cricket as much as I do,' Stokes replies. And then he adds that he thinks that the series has 'captivated so many new fans and attracted a new audience towards the game'. It's a bold claim, worth pursuing.

Across the 23 days when play occurred, the turnstiles clicked on about 470,000 occasions at the five grounds. Many of those attending would, of course, have been serial offenders. That number represents about 70,000 more than the number of actual people who attend games in any week of football's Premier League and roughly double the numbers who watch in the Championship, England's second tier of football. We're maybe not comparing like with like – a special day out at the Test as opposed to (for me) dutiful weekly attendance – but it's a reasonable starting point when talking about reach and appeal. When it comes to broadcast media, figures tell a clearer story.

Sky registered an average of just over 877,000 per day over the five Test matches. Their best day was the final day at the Oval – on a working Monday – where numbers peaked at 1.2 million. By contrast, on the final day of the Ashes at the Oval in 2005, with Channel 4 broadcasting Test cricket free-to-air, numbers peaked at 7.4 million. Just before Zak Crawley started making hay on the Friday of the fourth Test, England's women footballers were watched by a daytime audience of 4.2 million. Sky's average weekly viewing for Premier League games, discounting those broadcast to bars and other public spaces, is just under 2 million. England's football World Cup quarter-final against France was watched live by 23 million.

There's a perfectly sound argument that some of these comparisons don't bear close scrutiny. For example, much of Test cricket takes place during working days, with people checking scores and watching highlights on a range of platforms. BBC's *Test Match Special*, along with its website showing retrospective clips of the action, registered over six million hits during the course of the series. There is also a range of media providers issuing content unlawfully on which the live action can be accessed – although this applies similarly to football. But dress it up how you will, even at its most popular, cricket has to work very hard to fight for its place in the frenetic world of broadcast media. For the foreseeable future, its governing bodies will never have access to the sort of funding that will enable them to address this. Only through widening participation in the game and by, as a consequence, enhancing its profile and popularity can it prevent cricket, particularly in its longest form, from being anything other than a fringe activity.

And yet, for all these problems and misgivings, the excitement, drama and endless talking points of those 45 days of cricket in June and July of 2023 provided a welcome chance to bask and bathe in the brilliance of the game we love. Heroes and villains; brilliance and blunders; twists of fate and twists of ligaments; retirements and recalls and the very epitome of glorious uncertainty. What's more, exhausted as we may have been by following the action in those captivating days, it is worth pointing out that, as a mark of England's development as a team, at no point in the entire series did they once find themselves 29/3.

## Chapter 13

# Cricket, race, class and money: enduring challenges, evasive solutions

*Some sins do bear their privilege on earth*

Bastard: *King John*

IN JULY 1995, *Wisden Cricket Monthly* allocated a 2,000-word article entitled 'Is it in the blood?' to the writer, Robert Henderson. Written with prim stuffiness and an overuse of arch, rhetorical questions, it is redolent of thousands of prolix, bumptious letters of complaint that were once the mainstay of local free-sheet newspapers. But on this occasion, the object of Henderson's irritation is not the feckless council who won't cut the verges or empty his bins. His concern is the naivety of those who think that someone with darker skin and with some heritage beyond the British Isles might not be giving it his all when representing his 'adopted country'.

Tempting as it is to snigger at Henderson's debased view of the world, it really is no laughing matter. He probably regards himself as unfortunate that he didn't have the term 'woke' at his disposal back in the 90s, but this doesn't prevent his taking aim at that enduring target for those who lament the passing of a non-existent golden age – the liberal elite. 'An Asian or negro raised in England will, according to the liberal, feel exactly the same pride and identification with the place as a white man,' he complains, before assuring us that 'the reality is somewhat different.' The fact is, according to Henderson, that there really must be something brimming in the blood of these fellows. 'It is even possible,' he goes on to consider, 'that part of a coloured England-qualifying player feels satisfaction (perhaps unconsciously) at seeing England humiliated, because of post-imperial myths of oppression and exploitation.' You can be confident that you're dealing with the semi-deranged when slavery and dispossession are dismissed as a 'post-imperial myth'.

Unsurprisingly, Black England players of the time took unkindly to Henderson's clumsy racist bluster. Devon Malcolm and Phil DeFreitas issued libel writs against the magazine and these resulted in speedy settlements and significant compensation. Chris Lewis and Gladstone Small also threatened action, with their cases being settled out of court. The magazine's editor, David Frith, immediately distanced himself from Henderson's views, citing a journalistic duty not to shy away from a contested and controversial area of the game as the reason for allowing him to express his opinion in the first place.

The following year, with the publication of the full *Wisden* almanack, its editor, Matthew Engel, acknowledged that the magazine was 'under the same ultimate ownership' and that Henderson's article had instigated a 'particularly painful episode for us'. Like Frith, he is keen to dissociate himself from the ideas in the piece. 'The Henderson thesis,' he confirms, 'is, in essence, piffle ... he is not qualified to analyse anyone's subconscious.' Engel goes on to condemn as 'abhorrent and unthinkable' any suggestion that an England team should discriminate against Black players. So, that's all sorted then. A possibly over-generous application of the principle of press freedom, due compensation paid to victims and a heartfelt post-facto recognition of distasteful viewpoints. Let's move on, shall we? It was all some time ago, after all.

Which would be the wrong thing to do on two counts. First, the article may have been written a quarter of a century ago, but by then issues of race equality were hardly the niche concern of the early 1960s, when British society had only just started to adjust to the introduction of those who had accepted the invitation to live and work in the UK. How dull must the antennae of Frith and his colleagues have been not to have realised the loony tune that Henderson was playing? Quite how tin-eared, even back then, did they need to be for a reference to the 'generally resentful and separatist mentality of the West Indian-descended population of England' not to have taken them aback for just a moment? When he invokes the need to pick a team that 'is unequivocally English so that the majority can infect any fainthearts with their pride', did that not elicit the faintest tremor of concern? Or his final assertion that the 'desire to succeed [is] instinctive, a matter of biology'? Not even the triggering of the quietest alarm?

This tone-deafness in the offices of cricket's most venerated journal demonstrates the intrinsic, embedded nature of the values and attitudes that too many at the top of the game have inherited. In the three decades that followed, they have chosen not to mount any serious challenge to them.

The revelations of the Rafiq affair demonstrated how this unopposed hegemony of thought and outlook had sunk deep roots into the game. If Rafiq hadn't found out already by the summer of 2020, when the fallout from his interview with Taha Hashim made its first ripples, he could have done worse than dig out the history of this embarrassing display of bone-headedness from some of the doyens of the game.

There's a second, very contemporary reason why the Henderson affair shouldn't be chucked in history's wastebin. In September 2021, Sky first aired its illuminating documentary *You Guys Are History* – the title taken from the apparently apocryphal tale that Devon Malcolm's utterly ferocious spell of 9-57 against South Africa at the Oval in 1994 was inspired by events after he'd been hit by a bouncer from Fanie de Villiers. Unamused by the subsequent merriment of the fielders around him, Malcolm is said to have uttered the phrase, although he has always denied doing so.

The programme is fronted by Mark Butcher, who conducts affairs with admirable clarity and firmness of purpose, directed at exposing a dispiriting lack of advancement of players of Black heritage. It begins with a moment of sublime success for one such player – Jofra Archer at the World Cup Final of 2019. An England World Cup success with a Black man at the very centre of proceedings. That should be about as good as it gets. As the programme draws to its close, Archer himself muses on what an alternative universe might have looked like. He cites the social media abuse endured by the three young Black footballers who missed penalties in the 2021 Euro Final and suggests that it doesn't take too much imagination to think what would have happened had his final, crucial super over not resulted in an England win.

As it happens, he didn't even need to make an error on the field of play for the keyboard warriors to find something to peck away at.

At the height of summer in 2020, with England in the middle of a bubbled Test series against the West Indies, Archer broke the England team's quarantine rules and made an unauthorised visit to his flat in Hove. With fear and uncertainty about Covid at its height, and with cricket making some sort of effort to alleviate the boredom muffling all public life, it was an unconscionably stupid thing to have done – and it didn't take Archer long to realise this and apologise accordingly. Given that, as with any halfway prominent Black sportsperson, racist abuse was already sutured into his life, it was unsurprising that it spiked again following this misdemeanour. All of which played into the underpinning stereotype of the lazy, feckless Black man – and which the player himself refused to ignore.

In a press statement he explained that, 'Since Wilfried Zaha, the Crystal Palace footballer, was abused by a 12-year-old online, I drew a line and I will not allow anything to pass, so I have forwarded on my complaints to the ECB and that will go through the correct process.' The board made the correct noises, but it was left to one of the game's most respected voices to speak out with the greatest force. Jason Gillespie, the first indigenous Australian to play for his country and one of the most sought-after coaches in the world, talked of being 'pretty disappointed with some of the criticism levelled at Jofra'. Referencing 'a few gold chains' and a 'different hairstyle', Gillespie expressed impatience with those who 'assume that he doesn't care or he's not putting the effort in. Nothing could be further from the truth – the kid lives and breathes cricket.'

None of which is to suggest that the game's current authorities fail to recognise the need to tackle racism or to take it seriously. Throughout this book there has been no suggestion that cricket is failing to consider how it might sustain itself in a world that looks very different from the cloistered traditions and fustiness of the Long Room. But if the members now know that it's better to bite back comments about fellows with a tinge, when it comes to matters of class privilege, ground will not be ceded so readily. In June 2022, they were put to the test and were not found wanting when it came to preserving what was rightfully theirs.

It was left to the chief executive of MCC, Guy Lavender, to announce that Lord's would no longer host the annual match between the schools of Eton and Harrow. The decision, he explained, had not been 'taken lightly', adding reassuringly that 'it did not arise as a result of anxiety to kowtow to the woke police.' I don't really think those language choices require further comment. The game had not been scrapped forever: it might return for anniversaries or special occasions. The decision, said Lavender, had been made in order 'to ensure the highest quality pitches for professional cricket and to make Lord's more accessible to a wider range of players and extend playing opportunities to more teams instead of letting a bunch of posh buffoons gambol around on it in order to further cement their already bloated sense of self-worth'. No, of course he didn't say the last bit.

Since the end of the Second World War, Eton has produced one Test cricketer. George Mann played for England on seven occasions from 1948, captaining his country each time. Etonian Matthew Fleming played in 11

ODIs and Alex Loudon turned out for one. Gary Ballance, who featured ingloriously earlier in this book, probably tips the scales in Harrow's favour with his 24 Tests and 18 ODIs (and his one appearance since for Zimbabwe), but it's fair to say that neither school has been a hotbed of Test cricketers in the same way it has for the production of prime ministers of varying quality – 27 in all, with Eton providing 20. The answer to the question about why this lack of cricketing prowess merits a game at Lord's is lodged deeply in class composition and the unchallenged resort to half-baked notions of tradition that have bedevilled cricket for well over a century.

Days after the latest Etonian incumbent at Downing Street handed over the keys to Liz Truss for her short but calamitous tenancy, the good members had established the Historic Fixtures Group at Lord's, the HFG, issuing a statement that the removal of the Eton–Harrow game was 'tantamount to cutting down oak trees to accommodate saplings'. Quite what Lord Byron, who had played in the inaugural fixture in 1805, would have made of the metaphor, we can only surmise. More certain is that the HFG won the day in spectacular and rapid style. The fixture was immediately reinstated, albeit with a commitment to review in 2027, with the HFG acknowledging that, at some point, Eton and Harrow might just have to take their chances in the more inclusive Road to Lord's initiative. All the same, it's not difficult to imagine a note of exasperation in the comments of MCC chair Bruce Carnegie-Brown who observed that the episode 'demonstrates that we are listening to our members who want us to play our part in making cricket a game for all and to respect our history and traditions'.

So it was that on a chilly, drizzly day in mid-May, Harrow prevailed by four runs in front of a cavernous Lord's in a game that, according to the school's website, 'will go down as one of the most exciting duels ... in the 218-year history' of the fixture. Blazered and braying, the schoolboy spectators were something of a pre-reconfiguration of the standard audience for the signature events of the English summer. That is to say, signature events as framed through the lens of the privileged and financially comfortable. And white.

The Hollies Stand and the Western Terrace may bring a more demotic and transgressive flavour to Test cricket, but in the days that followed the drama at Edgbaston, the spectacle of the English well-to-do at leisure told the enduring story of disparity of race and class. During the woozy days of long, often sun-baked evenings, crowds paid huge money to be seen at Ascot and Glyndebourne. From Lord's, well-heeled punters could have taken their credit cards down next day to sample the joys of Wimbledon. At Glastonbury, almost exclusively white crowds karaoked along to their heroes and heroines who, at least, presented a rather more diverse picture of society than their doting admirers. There is a saving grace that some of these occasions were free-to-air; Test cricket, other than its increasingly niche product of *TMS* on radio, remained stubbornly hidden from the public gaze.

Two days after Zak Crawley had appeased the gods of sporting symmetry by pushing Pat Cummins's cut over the boundary rope to seal Australia's victory in the first Test, society – and cricket – acknowledged Windrush Day, 75 years after the first arrivals from the Caribbean docked at Tilbury. Media outlets retold the important stories of determination, resilience and accomplishment and, above all, of the almost ubiquitous racism that tainted the lives and chances of so many new arrivals. Plenty of these transmissions referenced the importance of cricket as an element that played a part in bolstering the self-esteem of those struggling to build a new life. Although jostling for space with Lord Kitchener's calypso rendition of London being the place for him, Lord Beginner's paeon to the feats of Ramadhin and Valentine, those little pals of his who took 18-279 between them to win the Lord's Test of 1950, still edged its occasional way in. More common were shots of triumphant and boisterous crowds celebrating the Blackwash – the 5-0 series win – at the Oval in 1984.

Cricket clubs were keen to acknowledge the anniversary. The satellite receivers of the board at Yorkshire had been particularly carefully tuned. Its website talked of how it 'proudly supports the Windrush 75 campaign and its celebration of the legacy and impact of an extraordinary generation of migrants'. It pointed, in particular, to the work of ACE in Sheffield schools and to a range of events, all with inclusion and participation at their centre, with which it was associated. There is no doubting the good intentions of the sentiments from a bruised institution, but it was left to two former pros to set a harder edge to the issue.

On the website of the Professional Cricketers' Association, Alex Tudor expressed the view that occasional events like Black History Month don't cut it in terms of addressing discrimination. 'I've said it before that I don't agree with Black History Month just being a month,' he explained, going on to suggest that combatting prejudice 'should be taught throughout the year'. He went on to reference the brave and outstanding work of Michael Holding in not shying away from the importance of the death of George Floyd and the growth of the Black Lives

Matter movement. In this, Tudor was in accord with another ex-England quick.

Writing on the website of the ECB, Devon Malcolm also paid tribute to Holding, before going on to express the view that 'something changed after George Floyd's murder. All over the world people of all races have drawn a line and are no longer afraid to speak out and fight for justice for a human being who lost his life because of the colour of his skin.' In the uncompromising nature of these views, and, it could be argued, in the willingness of two of the game's staider institutions to give them a platform, Tudor and Malcolm's comments suggest that English cricket may just be growing up a little in terms of its conversations about race. Against these developments, the world of those who dash for the bolthole of banter and selective deafness seems ever more ludicrous.

And if all of that sounds a touch harsh on a generally well-meaning constituency of county members and club stalwarts, then maybe we can cut them a little slack. If more serious bodies charged with running society exhibited constant failings when it came to race and class, wasn't it a bit too much to ask cricket to do so?

The period between the drama at Edgbaston and the fury at Lord's evinced much that brought cricket, race and politics to the fore. First, a constant wound on the body of English criminal law was scratched and exposed again. The episode that had prompted the introduction of the notion of institutionalised racism into public life, the inept investigation into the murder of Stephen Lawrence in 1993, threw up yet another example of just how maladroit the actions of the Metropolitan Police had been. A new suspect, since deceased, was identified. Evidence and accounts had always suggested that there had been six, rather than five, attackers, but the Met had failed to pursue this line of inquiry. Acknowledging that this had been 'a significant and regrettable error', the police also confirmed the investigation was no longer active.

The original inquiry into the Met's handling of the case had found that it had been 'marred by a combination of professional incompetence, institutional racism and a failure of leadership'. It's worth taking a moment to reflect on this judgement and to consider the manifold ways in which it could be applied to public life in the UK.

Tainted as it has been by one former prime minister who has become the byword for cowardice, selfishness and dishonesty, another who took just weeks to break the economy and yet another floundering so far out of his depth that we might expect him to appear in public wearing a rubber ring, this mistrust hardly comes as a surprise. A King's College study in 2022 found that public trust in parliament had fallen from 46% (alarming enough) in 1990 to 23% in 2022; a 24% approval rate of government puts the UK in the bottom third of all countries; 13% of people trust the press, which is the same as for political parties. All percentages have significantly diminished in the last 30 years. These are numbers that speak of deep-seated problems: cricket and its governance can only ever be a reflection of the society in which it exists and operates. Asking it to address its challenges in isolation is as unfair as it is unrealistic.

Which is not to say that when it did eventually appear, some three months behind schedule, the report of the Independent Commission for Equality in Cricket (ICEC) didn't take its best shot at doing so. Published just before the start of the Lord's Test, it made headline news. On a personal note, I was both delighted and surprised to hear the voice of Chevy Green from ACE, assigned to do the media rounds, giving his reaction on one of the prime slots on the Radio 4 *Today* programme. I message him immediately about his new media star profile; I will see him the next day to watch his boys in action. For now, however, it's time to see what sort of job the commission has done.

The immediate contrast between its document and that of the Pollyannaish ECB publications is striking. Entitled *Holding a Mirror up to Cricket* and presented in sober and serious dark green, its 317 pages are devoid of glossy photos or barking mission statements. The language throughout is unequivocal and unforgiving. In her foreword, the chair, Cindy Butts, makes it clear that nobody is going to be let off the hook. 'There remains a stark reality,' she states, 'that cricket is not a game for everyone.' What's more, she insists, this report is pointless without subsequent actions. 'The building of a truly equitable sport will not follow passively' just from reading it. What needs to happen is that, 'The game will need to apply a steadfast commitment and relentless vigilance to ensure that the policies, practice and systems are reformed and embedded into all aspects of cricket.' And lest the message be lost, we are reminded that 'what is needed now is leadership' and that this needs to be 'driven forward by the ECB and others'. None of this will happen until there is 'an acceptance of the widespread discrimination and structural barriers which have existed and continue to exist within cricket'. In a further echo of a societal mistrust of officialdom, the report draws attention to the reluctance of many people, particularly of Black and South Asian current or former players, to contribute. Such reticence arises 'from a distrust of governing organisations, concerns about confidentiality or suspicion about our true independence from the ECB'.

It continues in this unflinching way. Unapologetically placing its work in a historical and political context, it is true to its word in holding up a mirror to the issues of class and race that are part of cricket's history. It acknowledges outdated attitudes to women and girls. It talks of elitism and of how, in schools, the game is now the preserve of the private sector. It identifies barriers to participation that are structural and endemic and of how cricket has failed Black communities. Where it uses brief commentary from contributors, these are stark and uncomfortable. 'I have been told that a lady cannot be a good umpire, I should go back home – women's cricket is shit [and women] can't make decisions.' Another respondent talks of how 'all the stories that Azeem Rafiq talked about, they all happened to me – all the abuse, the isolation, the hatred'. A parent talks about how 'the size of your wallet determines if they are going to progress or not … it's not a sport for everyone, but a privileged few'.

It is grim, but entirely unsurprising reading. The report finishes with 44 recommendations, the first of which manages to take a quick snapshot of both its brief and the problems exposed. 'We recommend that the ECB makes an unqualified public apology for its own failings and those of the game it governs … [it] should acknowledge that racism, sexism, elitism and class-based discrimination have existed, and still exist, in the game, and recognise the impact on victims of discrimination.'

It goes on to suggest that this 'should include, in particular, a direct apology for the ECB's and the wider game's historic failures in relation to women's and girls' cricket and its failure to adequately support Black cricket in England and Wales'.

And to be fair, such an apology was immediate. ECB chair, Richard Thompson, seeing the writing stamped on the wall, took the only path open. 'On behalf of the ECB and wider leadership of the game, I apologise unreservedly to anyone who has ever been excluded from cricket or made to feel they don't belong.' He went on to make all the right noises about action plans to be on stream within three months and of the 'absolute commitment' of the board to ensure that cricket would become 'the most inclusive sport in England and Wales'. You wouldn't need to be a genius to imagine that Richard wasn't enjoying the most comfortable of days. Perhaps if he'd joined me the following morning, he'd have been feeling a touch more chipper.

I am to join Chevy Green and his ACE cricketers who are playing in a four-team knockout T20 tournament. I arrive late, numb and flubbery from the dentist, at the resplendent playing fields of Berkhamsted School in Hertfordshire. I park up and take in the manicured outfield and the spacious, modern, airy pavilion. Spectators lounge on the balcony while some recline in deck chairs on the boundary. On the far side of the playing area, huge marquees have been erected for the evening's forthcoming prom and an accomplished musical rehearsal wafts out a mellow soundtrack. An upmarket 'street food' van plies its trade as lunchtime approaches. The teams look magnificent in their trim, coloured clothing and the elegant electronic scoreboard whirrs as the pink cricket ball flies. But I'm slightly baffled. Neither of the teams out on the field of play or chilling around the pavilion resemble the young men I'd seen at the Oval in January.

And that's because they're playing on the adjacent pitch. The outfield is equally immaculate if marginally smaller and slightly irregular in places; the pavilion is not quite as grand, but incomparably spacious and better appointed than those of most cricket clubs; the whole playing area is fringed with mature trees and sturdy but tasteful netting which ensures that balls skipping beyond the boundary are easily and immediately retrievable. When I take a stroll later on, I find that there's one further similar playing area for cricket and then, on an extensive perimeter, there are yet more playing fields incorporating an athletics' track and synthetic pitches. Non-boarding places at the school are available for just over £25,000 a year, while fees for boarders come in at just over £41,000.

When I locate ACE, I find that they're making a mess of defending a total of 127 in their first game. Chevy is disgruntled in a subdued way, but coach Donovan Miller seems less forgiving of his players' carelessness and, in particular, their having failed to use their full 20-over allocation. He's a man who should be heeded. His coaching pedigree has been forged in the Caribbean Premier League, county cricket and as part of the support team for England's triumphant 2109 World Cup campaign. ACE's first opponents, Buckinghamshire under-18s, knock off the runs with four balls to spare. I am not party to the dressing-room debrief, but it becomes clear that Miller has hammered home the need for greater diligence in the next game.

In the interlude, I chat to parents. I find one with whom I have some tangential connection, with his having played for a side in my local ambit, St Albans West Indians. With no prompting from me, he reels off tales of discrimination on and off the field of play – docked points for contesting umpiring decisions, for failing to field a full XI, for incomplete player registrations – which he is convinced are rules that have been enforced in a discriminatory and needlessly draconian way. Similarly, he feels that his talented son has not been given due credit at county level, which is why he has found his way to ACE.

With other parents, the conversation turns, inevitably, to our immediate surroundings and the way these contrast with the facilities available to those in the state school system. Just as inevitable are their observations that without their own time, transport and money, cricket would be a game that would be beyond the reach and experience of their children. As ever, it has been their own connections to clubs that has been the route to the game for their offspring. The ICEC report is comprehensive and unwavering in its attempt to paint the picture of the game as it is, but had it wanted a microcosmic representation of its concerns, it would have found one in this clipped, emerald field in Hertfordshire while, some 30 miles further south, England's right-arm-over dependables failed to take advantage of having inserted their opponents at Lord's.

Donovan and Chevy's boys aren't going to get fooled again. In their losers' final against Hertfordshire, they bat first and biff the pink ball to all points of the compass. I'm not quite sure what to make of the instructions from anxious parents. Advice about not letting the bowler settle when the ball is flying over the ropes with unstinting regularity, or, my favourite, an imprecation not to do anything stupid now, with the score approaching 200 after 17 overs, seem misplaced if well-meaning. The scoreboard on this outer playing area – had they beaten Bucks, they'd have been on the main square – doesn't display individual scores, which is a shame. Having batted with a mixture of elegance, great awareness and with the occasional rustic smear, opener Jordan is unaware that he is on 98 when he plays a searing, flat drive over extra cover, only for long off to sprint round to take a brilliantly timed catch just inside the boundary. He seems remarkably composed when he returns to his mates communicating his unhappy fate, and coach Donovan is equally unperturbed: 'The right shot for the team,' he confirms. I can't help but think I've just heard an echo of Stokes and Buttler's no-regrets mantra.

Hertfordshire stutter from the start in the face of some ferocious fast bowling and they never recover. Donovan has a few quiet grumbles about naïve field placing, but the underlying regret is that they've missed the chance to be in the final proper. A fellow coach comes to chat and tells Chevy that he believes ACE are the best team there. Chevy later tells me that he has already been approached by a senior representative from the school who, immediately recognising the importance of ICEC, wants to talk about ways in which they can provide support and access. It's also clear that many of the players know each other and get along. There appears to be a genuine sense of the possibility of a cricket community emerging: Cindy Butts, her committee and Richard Thompson could afford themselves the beginnings of a smile.

The ICEC report lists 79 organisations that had contributed to its findings. Among these there are bodies that may not have benefited from the recognition afforded to ACE because of some of its high-profile leaders but which, nevertheless, work to address cricket's problems with equality and discrimination. None of those individuals would suggest that a good-natured but competitive cricket tournament, where the players looked more like members of modern society than their international counterparts, is anything other than a welcome but superficial sign of some progress. But to repeat the point, and to invoke C.L.R. James's famous observation – 'what do they know of cricket who only cricket know' – asking cricket alone to rectify the wrongs of the wider world is insupportable.

At the heart of the ICEC report is the observation that 'we ... found that elitism alongside deeply rooted and widespread forms of institutional and structural racism, sexism and class-based discrimination continue to exist across the game'. No equivocation, no excuses, no softened language. Compare and contrast. In 2022, the government instigated its own commission into Race and Ethnic Disparities. Its conclusion that 'we no longer see a Britain where the system is deliberately rigged against ethnic minorities' was welcomed with glee by ministers, proudly asserting that 'we're already one of the fairest countries in the world'.

Beyond Whitehall, the report, its findings and its subsequent high-level approval was met with a mixture of bewilderment, rage and tired resignation. The UN working group of Experts on People of African Descent categorically rejected and condemned it; UK public health experts called it 'divorced from reality'; the mother of Stephen Lawrence said it pushed back the fight against racism '20 years or more'; the union of academics said it demonstrated 'an astonishing complacency'. Cindy Butts, Brendan Barber, Michelle Moore, Michael Collins and Zafar Ansari did what politicians singularly failed to do: look a problem square in the eye to identify it and so give themselves a chance of solving it. They'd be entitled to ask for significantly better moral leadership and courage from their political masters to help them on their way.

And so, we return, almost inevitably, to the words of C.L.R. James in the epigram at the start of this book. He talks of 'old barriers breaking down' and of how 'in the inevitable integration into a national community' it will be 'sport, and particularly cricket' that will play a great role in building a better society. As Pat Cummins tucked the urn into his suitcase, as the Yorkshire board thanked their lucky stars for the rapidity of their access to Test match incomes, as Azeem Rafiq contemplated his part in the history of the modern game and as Chevy organised and arranged, cricket could rest on the laurels of two months' worth of remarkable competition. Asking it to solve global problems is as unfair as it is stupid. Hoping that it'll have a go at doing so isn't such an outlandish hope.

# Afterword

*The rest is silence*

Hamlet: *Hamlet*

WHEREVER I'VE drawn on the work of other writers, journalists and researchers, I've acknowledged this explicitly in the text. I'm grateful for their endeavours and hope that they'll be happy to draw on my own efforts in their turn.

I've deliberately not clogged the text with footnotes. Any reference to a report, public document, press release, TV news item or tweeted comment is available with a ten-second search and a quick click. Similarly, episodes and events from the games mentioned are just as easily accessible from online platforms – but I'll warn readers that you can lose entire days once you start going down that rabbit hole.

Because you may want to know, I've used the lines from Shakespeare at the start of chapters because I like them, and they seem to fit. I'd like to tell you that they stand as a clever metaphor for the inevitable demise of flawed heroes or the timelessness of great ideas like Test cricket, but that's simply not true. They're just a bit of fun.

I started planning and writing this book late in 2022, so there's been an element of running to catch up throughout the process. Despite my best efforts, some of what's been covered will have been overtaken by events, principally, as I mention in the disclaimer at the start, England's 50-over meltdown in the autumn of 2023. All I can say is that I've tried not to let anything of major significance slip though the net. I know that I'll definitely have annoyed some of you by omitting something you consider of central importance. As I said right at the start, this was always meant to be a political book and so I'd be amazed – and a touch disappointed – if there are some of you who think I'm not fit to be out on my own. You can let me know via my website: I promise to respond as long as you're not in obvious need of specialised help.

# About the author

Jon Berry is a retired teacher and academic who writes widely about education, sport and politics – sometimes all three at once. He lives in Hertfordshire but, in the embodiment of the triumph of hope over experience, retains his season ticket for Birmingham City. He volunteers with refugee charities, hacks and swears his way round the golf course and works on being a decent husband, father and grandfather.

www.jonberrywriter.co.uk

# By the same author

**Sport**

*The Armchair Fan's Guide to the Qatar World Cup*

*Project Restart – how football came out of lockdown*

*Hugging Strangers – the frequent lows and occasional highs of football fandom*

**Politics and society**

*Brutish Necessity – A Black Life Forgotten*

*Boomeranting*

**Education**

*Putting the test in its Place*

*Teachers Undefeated*